Guess What!

Activity Book 5
with Online Resources

British English

Lynne Marie Robertson
Series Editor: Lesley Koustaff

CAMBRIDGE
UNIVERSITY PRESS

CAMBRIDGE
UNIVERSITY PRESS & ASSESSMENT

Shaftesbury Road, Cambridge CB2 8EA, United Kingdom

One Liberty Plaza, 20th Floor, New York, NY 10006, USA

477 Williamstown Road, Port Melbourne, VIC 3207, Australia

314–321, 3rd Floor, Plot 3, Splendor Forum, Jasola District Centre, New Delhi – 110025, India

103 Penang Road, #05-06/07, Visioncrest Commercial, Singapore 238467

Cambridge University Press & Assessment is a department of the University of Cambridge.

We share the University's mission to contribute to society through the pursuit of education, learning and research at the highest international levels of excellence.

www.cambridge.org
Information on this title: www.cambridge.org/9781107545427

© Cambridge University Press & Assessment 2016

First published 2016

40 39 38 37 36 35 34 33 32 31 30 29 28 27 26 25

Printed in Malaysia by Vivar Printing

A catalogue record for this publication is available from the British Library

ISBN 978-1-107-54542-7 Activity Book with Online Resources Level 5
ISBN 978-1-107-54539-7 Pupil's Book Level 5
ISBN 978-1-107-12320-5 Teacher's Book with DVD Level 5
ISBN 978-1-107-54547-2 Class Audio CDs Level 5
ISBN 978-1-107-54549-6 Presentation Plus DVD-ROM Level 5
ISBN 978-1-107-54570-0 Teacher's Resource and Tests CD-ROM Levels 5-6

Additional resources for this publication at www.cambridge.org/guesswhat

Cambridge University Press & Assessment has no responsibility for the persistence or accuracy of URLs for external or third-party internet websites referred to in this publication, and does not guarantee that any content on such websites is, or will remain, accurate or appropriate. Information regarding prices, travel timetables, and other factual information given in this work is correct at the time of first printing but Cambridge University Press & Assessment does not guarantee the accuracy of such information thereafter.

Contents

Around the world

1 Look and write the words on the map.

> hinaC   lriBaz   het detiUn asettS   sirsuaR   boloCaim
> xcMeoi   latIy   eraFnc   ~~het Unedit modginK~~   naSip

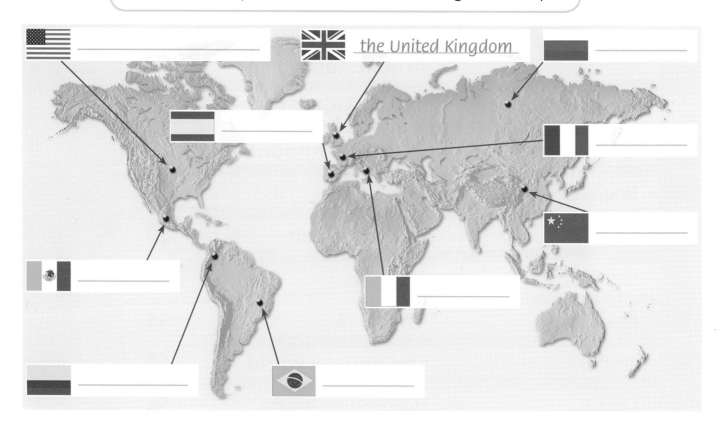

the United Kingdom

2 (Think) Look at activity 1. Answer the questions.

1 Which country hasn't got red in its flag?

_____Brazil_____

2 Which two countries have got red, white and green flags?

_____   _____

3 Which two countries have got red and yellow flags?

_____   _____

4 Which four countries have got red, white and blue flags?

_____   _____   _____   _____

My picture dictionary ➡ Go to page 84: Write the new words.

3 Complete the questions and answers. Use the words in brackets.

Juan (Mexico)

1 __Where__ are you __from__ ?

I'm __from Mexico__ .

Maria (Italy)

2 _____'s she _____ ?

She's _____ .

Bo and Hai (China)

3 _____ are they _____ ?

They're _____ .

Oliver (the United Kingdom)
and his father (Colombia)

4 _____'s Oliver's _____ ?

He's _____ .

4 Look at activity 3. Write the questions and answers.

1 __Is__ Oliver __from__ Mexico? __No, he isn't.__

2 _____ Bo and Hai _____ China? _____

3 _____ Juan _____ Mexico? _____

4 _____ Maria _____ Colombia? _____

5 _____ Oliver's father _____ Colombia? _____

5 My World Write the questions and answers.

1 __Is__ your English teacher __from__ Russia? _____

2 __Where__ is your English teacher __from__ ? _____

3 _____ is your favourite singer _____ ? _____

4 _____ is your favourite food _____ ? _____

6 Put the words in order. Then match.

1 you / were / When / born?
   When were you born? [b]

2 were / Where / born? / you
   _____ [ ]

3 Hana / was / born? / When
   _____ [ ]

4 born? / Where / she / was
   _____ [ ]

5 When / born? / were / Alex and Ani
   _____ [ ]

6 they / born? / were / Where
   _____ [ ]

a They were born in Russia.
b I was born on the 9th of September.
c She was born in Mexico.
d I was born in Italy.
e They were born on the 21st of February.
f She was born on the 18th of November.

7 Read and complete the questions and answers.

Name	Date of birth	Place of birth
Megan	1st April, 2005	Colombia
Tom	23rd July, 2006	the United Kingdom
Juan	7th December, 2005	France

1 ___When___ was Tom ___born___ ? He _was born on the_ 23 _rd_ of July, 2006.
2 _____ was Megan _____ ? She _____ in Colombia.
3 _____ Tom _____ ? _____ in the United Kingdom.
4 _____ Juan _____ ? _____ in _____ .
5 _____ Megan _____ ? _____ on _____ .
6 _____ Juan _____ ? _____ on _____ .

8 (My World) Answer the questions.

1 Where is your family from?   *My family is from* _____
2 Are you from Italy?   _____
3 Where was your father born?   _____
4 When was your mother born?   _____

9 Think **Read the story again and number.**

 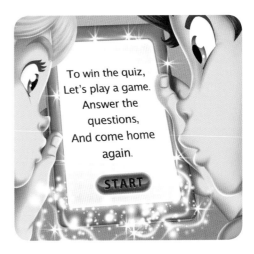

To win the quiz,
Let's play a game.
Answer the
questions,
And come home
again.

START

☐ **a** They want to do the World Quiz together. The first question is about Colombia.

☐ **b** They go to the reading room to email Ruby's penpal. But it isn't the reading room!

☐ **c** Ruby can email her penpal. Her penpal is from Colombia.

1 **d** Jack and Ruby are at the library. They see a quiz.

10 **Read and write *true* or *false*.**

1 Ruby thinks the quiz sounds fun. ___*true*___

2 Ruby and Jack don't know which city in Colombia has a flower festival. _____

3 Ruby's penpal is from Russia. _____

4 They want to email Jack's sister. _____

5 They want to win the quiz. _____

11 My World **What can you do to show the value: try new things?**

1 _You can eat new foods._

2 _____

3 _____

4 _____

5 _____

Story   Value   **7**

Skills: *Reading*

12 **Read Tim's email and circle the correct answers.**

Hi Luis,

How are you? My name's Tim. I was born on the 28th May, 2008. I'm from the United Kingdom, but my father's from Spain.

We have fun festivals in Cambridge. The Strawberry Fair is in June. It's on Saturday the 6th. There are music, dance, and circus acts. In July, there's a big music festival called the Cambridge Folk Festival. The music is fantastic.

Where are you from in Spain? Do you know the festival called Tamborrada? It's in San Sebastian, Spain. People play music on drums. It sounds like fun. I'd like to go someday. Please write and tell me about Spain.

Your penpal, Tim

Tamborrada, San Sebastian, Spain

Cambridge Folk Festival, Cambridge, UK

1 Where's Tim's father from?
- **a** Cambridge
- **b** the United Kingdom
- **c** Spain

2 When is Strawberry Fair?
- **a** 6th of June
- **b** in Cambridge
- **c** in autumn

3 Which festival is in July in Cambridge?
- **a** Strawberry Fair
- **b** the Folk Festival
- **c** the Circus Festival

4 Where's the drum festival?
- **a** the United Kingdom
- **b** San Sebastian, Spain
- **c** Cambridge

13 **(TIP)** **How to use capital letters.**

Use capital letters with:
names: *Tim, Luis*
festivals: *Cambridge Folk Festival*

towns and countries: *Cambridge, Spain*
days and months: *Saturday, May*

Read Tim's email again and circle all the capital letters. Then:

1 underline the names of people in red.
2 underline the towns and countries in blue.
3 draw boxes around the names of festivals in red.
4 draw boxes around the days and months in blue.

Skills: *Writing*

14   **Make notes about you and your town.**

About me.

Name: _____   Birthday: _____   Where I'm from: _____

About our town.

Name: _____   Country: _____

When to do and see things.

1   What:_____
    When: _____
    What it's like: _____

2   What:_____
    When: _____
    What it's like: _____

3   What:_____
    When: _____
    What it's like: _____

4   Ask your penpal a question.
    _____
    _____
    _____

15 **Write an email about your town to a penpal.**

Dear _____ ,

_____

_____

_____

_____

_____

_____

_____

_____

Your penpal,
(your name) _____

What are mosaics made of?

1 **Read and match the questions and answers.**

1 Where can we see mosaic art today? [d]

2 What are mosaics? [ ]

3 What are mosaic tiles made of? [ ]

4 What do artists use to put the tiles on cardboard? [ ]

a Pictures with many small tiles.

b Stones, ceramic, glass, paper.

c Glue.

d In places like train stations and shopping centres.

2 **Read and match. Then complete the sentences.**

a

b

c  [1]

1 This mosaic is made of lots of paper tiles. It shows a head, eyes and a ___mouth___ .

2 This mosaic is made of small, coloured tiles. It shows a head and legs.

It's a _____ .

3 This mosaic is made of marble. The mosaic is on a floor. The mosaic pattern shows

circles and _____ .

3 **Draw a mosaic for your home. Write three sentences about it.**

_____

_____

_____

_____

_____

Evaluation

1 **Complete the questions and answers.**

Hector: I ¹ _was_ ² _born_ ³ _on_ ⁴ _the_ 10th of October, 2005.

Gloria: Wow! I ⁵_____ ⁶_____ ⁷_____ ⁸_____ 10th of October, 2005 too.

Hector: We have the same ⁹_____ !

Gloria: ¹⁰_____ your friend Rosa ¹¹_____ Mexico, too?

Hector: No, she ¹²_____ . She's ¹³_____ the United States, but she ¹⁴_____ ¹⁵_____ in Columbia.

Hector: Where are you from, Gloria?

Gloria: I'm ¹⁶ _from_ the United Kingdom. But my grandmother's ¹⁷_____ China. Where are you ¹⁸_____ ?

Hector: I'm ¹⁹_____ Mexico.

Gloria: ²⁰_____ was Rosa ²¹_____ ?

Hector: She ²² _was_ ²³_____ ²⁴_____ ²⁵_____ 10th of October, 2006.

2 **Complete the sentences about this unit.**

✓ = I can …   ✗ = I can't …

☐ **1** … name ten countries.

☐ **2** … ask and answer questions about where people are from.

☐ **3** … ask and answer questions about when people are born.

☐ **4** … try new things.

☐ **5** … plan and talk about a tour of festivals using *I'd like to go to …* .

6 My favourite part of this unit is _____ .

1 Family and pets

1 **Read and circle the correct words.**

1 My cousin is good at Maths and English. He's ... .
   a clever   **b** sporty   **c** naughty

2 Jim's new puppy likes eating shoes. It's ... .
   a talkative   **b** hardworking   **c** naughty

3 Lena's parents always say hello. They're ... .
   a friendly   **b** shy   **c** artistic

4 I'm good at making models and painting. I'm ... .
   a artistic   **b** kind   **c** funny

5 Alex's brother doesn't like saying hello to me. He's ... .
   a kind   **b** clever   **c** shy

6 My friend Bill makes me laugh. He's ... .
   a sporty   **b** funny   **c** hardworking

7 My uncle tells lots of stories. He's ... .
   a talkative   **b** hardworking   **c** naughty

2 (Think) **Read and complete the sentences. Then write the names.**

                                                          Penny

1 Penny always talks on the phone. She's _____ _talkative_ _____ .

2 My cousin Mark is always mountain biking or bowling. He's _____ .

3 My uncle Arun is a businessman. He is always at his office. He likes working. He's _____ .

4 My aunt Jill works in a hospital. She gives people things. She's _____ .

 My picture dictionary → Go to page 85: Write the new words.

3 Look at Lee's chart. Then circle the correct words.

Lee   my sister, Jen

y-axis

10 ✓
   ✓
   ✓
   ✓
   ✓
5 ✓
   ✓
   ✓
   ✓
1 ✓

| friendly | talkative | naughty | shy | kind | hardworking |

x-axis

1   My sister, Jen, is **shyer/friendlier** than me.
2   I'm **more hardworking/naughtier** than my sister.
3   Jen is **kinder/more talkative** than me.
4   I'm **naughtier/kinder** than my sister.
5   My sister is **shyer/naughtier** than me.
6   I'm **shyer/more talkative** than my sister, Jen.

4 Look at activity 3. Complete the questions and answers.

1   Lee, is your sister _naughtier than_ you? (naughty)   _Yes, she is._
2   Lee, are you _____ your sister? (shy)   _____
3   Lee, are you _____ your sister? (talkative)   _____
4   Jen, is your brother _____ you? (kind)   _____
5   Jen, are you _____ your brother? (friendly)   _____
6   Jen, is your brother _____ you? (hardworking)   _____

5 **My World** Complete the questions and answers. Use the words in the box and your own ideas.

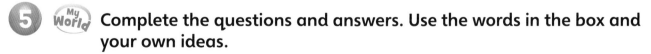

| sportier | more artistic | ~~shyer~~ | more talkative |

1   Are you _____ _shyer_ _____ than your friend?   _____
2   Are you _____ than your friend?   _____
3   Are you _____ than your friend?   _____

6 Complete the questions and answers.

1 _Who's younger_ , your sister or your parrot? (young)   My sister _is younger_ .
2 _____ , you or your parrot? (old)   My parrot _____ .
3 _____ , your cat or your dog? (quiet)   My cat _____ .
4 _____ , your dog or your parrot? (noisy) My parrot _____ .
5 _____ , you or your sister? (tall)   I _____ .
6 _____ , your sister or your father? (short) My sister _____ .

7 **My World** Write the questions and complete the answers. Then complete the table.

1 (artistic / you / your mother)
  Who's more artistic, you or your mother?   I _am_ .
2 (talkative / brother / sister)
  _____   My brother _____ .
3 (funny / your dog / your brother)
  _____   My dog _____ .
4 (quiet / your dog / your cat)
  _____   My cat _____ .
5 (tall / your father / your mother)
  _____   My father _____ .

artistic	quiet	hardworking	tall	sporty	talkative	funny
_me_		my mother		my sister		

8 (Think) **Read the story again. Match and then number.**

1	Jack and Ruby are _d_	**a**	answer the question.
	Sofia helps them _____	**b**	a message on a flower.
	Jack and Ruby read _____	**c**	than both of them today.
	They see Sofia. She is taller _____	**d**	at a flower festival.
	Sofia goes _____	**e**	with them.

9 **Read and circle the correct words.**

1 Jack and Ruby are in … .
  a Brazil   **b** China   **c** (Colombia)
2 Ruby thinks the message is from … .
  a her friend, Sofia   **b** the flowers   **c** the festival
3 Sofia can help them … .
  a be taller   **b** do the quiz   **c** be very clever
4 Sofia is taller today because she's … .
  a in the festival   **b** in Colombia   **c** playing the game
5 The flower festival is in … .
  a London   **b** Medellin   **c** Mexico City

10 **What can you do to show the value: learn about other cultures?**

1 _You can visit other countries._

2 _____

3 _____

4 _____

5 _____

Skills: *Reading*

11 Read and complete Camilla's report with the words in the box. Then write the names under the pictures.

~~clever~~   funnier   naughty   quieter   talkative   older   naughtier

Our Pets, by Camilla

My family likes animals. I have a grey pet rabbit called Skipper.
He knows his name. I think he's ¹_____*clever*_____ .
He comes when I call him. But sometimes he's
²_____ . He eats the carrots in our garden!

My cousin Sam has a pet parrot. Her name is Paco. She's
thirty-five years old – a lot ³_____ than Skipper.

Paco says things all the time. She's very
⁴_____ . She's also ⁵_____ than
my rabbit because she often makes us laugh. My pet rabbit is
a lot ⁶_____ than Paco. Skipper doesn't
say anything at all!

My brother also has a pet. It's a spider called Cob and
I don't like it! Sometimes my brother puts it in my hat.
My brother's ⁷_____ than Skipper!

_____

_____

_____

12 Look at activity 11. Answer the questions.

1 What does Skipper do that's naughty? _Skipper eats the carrots in Camilla's garden._

2 How old is Paco? _____

3 Who is funnier, Skipper or Paco? _____

4 Who is quieter, Skipper or Paco? _____

5 Who is naughtier, Skipper or Camilla's brother? _____

13 (TIP) **How to use *he*, *she* and *it* for pets.**

Use *he* or *she* when you know the name of the pet:
Skipper is a boy rabbit. He's friendly.   Paco is a girl parrot. She's smart.

Use *it* when you don't know the name of the pet and when you don't know if the animal is a boy or girl: *It's a spider called Cob and I don't like it.*

Read Camilla's report again and circle *he*, *she* and *it*.

Skills: *Writing*

  Make notes about two pets or animals you know.

Pet/Animal name:	What they're both like:	Pet/Animal name:
_____		_____
What it's like:	_____	What it's like:
_____	_____	_____
_____	_____	_____
_____	_____	_____

 Write a report about the two animals. Draw a picture.

Title: _____

_____

_____

_____

_____

_____

_____

_____

How do **ant families** work together?

1 **Read and write *true* or *false*.**

1 A family of ants is called a colony. _____true_____

2 Ants work together in groups. _____

3 Families of ants live in rooms. _____

4 All ant colonies have three queens. _____

5 Some worker ants bring stones to the nest. _____

2 **How are the animals working together?**

1 a They are taking leaves to the nest.
  b They are tidying the nest.
  c They are helping the queen ant.

2 a They are staying warm.
  b They are making a nest.
  c They are bringing food.

3 a They are looking for food for baby birds.
  b They are making a nest for baby birds.
  c They are watching the baby birds.

3 **Imagine that you are a worker ant. Write about your day and draw a picture.**

Evaluation

1 **Put the words in order. Then match.**

 Robert

 Gina

 Sam

 Olga

1   talkative / than / Robert, is / you? / Gina / more /
    Robert, is Gina more talkative than you?   [b]

2   than / Olga / taller / you? / Sam, is /
    _____   [   ]

3   is / Gina? / you / or / Sam, who / quieter, /
    _____   [   ]

4   Sam? / younger, Robert / or / Who is /
    _____   [   ]

a   is. / Sam /
    _____

b   No, / isn't. / she /
    No, she isn't.

c   is. / Gina /
    _____

d   is. / Yes, / she
    _____

2 **Look at activity 1 and complete the sentences. Use the words in the box.**

1   Robert: I'm _____ _older_ _____ than Sam.

2   Gina is _____ than Olga.

3   Olga: I'm _____ than Gina.

4   Sam is _____ than Olga.

> artistic   ~~old~~
> short   sporty

3 **Complete the sentences about this unit.**

✓ = I can …   ✗ = I can't …

[   ] **1** … say ten new words about people.

[   ] **2** … talk about people using words like *cleverer* and *more hardworking than*.

[   ] **3** … ask and answer questions using *Who's older, you or your brother?*

[   ] **4** … learn about other cultures.

[   ] **5** … think and write about someone I know.

6   In this unit, I found _____ more interesting than

_____ .

2 In the playground

1 Read and number the correct pictures. Then write.

1 You can do this to play a game or talk to someone. _use a mobile phone_

2 You can send a message to a friend this way. _____

3 You can do this in a baseball game.

_____

4 This is noisier than talking.

_____

5 You do this when something is funny.

_____

6 You can do this in sport, but it's not running or hopping. _____

a

b

c

d
1

e

f

2 Think Read and circle the odd ones out.

1 Do these things in the playground.
   a throw a ball   b (drop litter)   c skip   d laugh

2 Things you want to do with friends.
   a cry   b laugh   c text   d throw a ball

3 Things you can use a mobile phone to do.
   a help others   b text friends   c laugh   d hop

4 Don't do these things in the house.
   a drop litter   b help others   c shout   d throw a ball

 My picture dictionary → **Go to page 86: Write the new words.**

3 **Complete the sentences with *must* or *mustn't*.**

1 You ___mustn't___ use a mobile on a bike.

2 You _____ stop at a green traffic light.

3 You _____ stop at a red traffic light.

4 You _____ use a mobile phone in the cinema.

5 You _____ drop litter on the beach.

6 You _____ put litter in the bins.

4 **Read and write sentences with *must* or *mustn't*.**

1 We are at the cinema. We get a text. We want to text our friend.

   We ___mustn't___ text in the cinema.

2 We are on the street. We want to go to the shopping centre opposite us. There is a zebra crossing.

   We _____ use the zebra crossing.

3 We are at the museum. We see a painting. We want to touch it.

   We _____ touch the painting.

4 We are at a shopping centre. We want to run and shout with our friend.

   We _____ run and shout in the shopping centre.

5 After playing, we want to eat a sandwich.

   We _____ wash our hands before we eat.

5 **My World** **Write sentences using *must* or *mustn't* and the phrases in the boxes.**

> at home   in the classroom   ~~in the library~~   in the restaurant

1 _We must be quiet in the library._ .

2 _____ .

3 _____ .

4 _____ .

6 Put the words in order.

1 page, / Read / please. / this
Read this page, please.

2 biscuits, / me / Give / the / please.
_____

3 please. / the / Anna / Pass / glue,
_____

4 me / Bring / mobile phone, / please. / the
_____

5 photo, / please. / Show / the class / your
_____

6 Read / please. / the / me / story,
_____

7 Read and write the numbers from activity 6.

1 **Jill:** I've got a new book. It's got a funny story.
  Amy: ___6___

2 **Anna:** Oh, no! I need some glue.
  Teacher: _____
  Bill: Here you are, Anna.

3 **Mother:** I need to make a phone call. _____
  Mike: Here you are, Mum.

4 **Tom:** These biscuits are nice.
  Father: You mustn't eat biscuits before dinner, Tom. _____

5 **Jim:** I've got a photo of my new baby brother.
  Teacher: _____

6 **Teacher:** OK, class. Open your books at page 43. _____

8 **My World** Use the words to write instructions.

1 _Bring me the eraser, please._ (the eraser)

2 _____ (your photos)

3 _____ (the mobile phone)

4 _____ (your own idea)

9 (Think) **Read the story again. Then put the words in order and number.**

a mustn't / the / The children / monkey. / feed

[ ] _____

b Sofia / wants / to / give / the / monkey / some / fruit.

[1] _Sofia wants to give the monkey some fruit._____

c too. / is / Capu / in / school / the

[ ] _____

d school. / hide / in / They / a

[ ] _____

10 **Read and complete. Use the words in the box.**

| 1850   can take   classroom   monkey   mustn't   South America |

It's London, in ¹_____1850_____ . The children do something they ²_____

do. A man is angry. They run and hide in a ³_____ . Capu hides there too.

Capu is a capuchin ⁴_____ . He wants to go to ⁵_____ .

The children ⁶_____ Capu home.

11 (My World) **What can you do to show the value: be kind to animals?**

1 _You can take the dog for a walk._____

2 _____

3 _____

4 _____

5 _____

Story Value **23**

Skills: *Reading*

12 Read and complete the help letter with *must* or *mustn't*.

Jill can help!

Dear Jill,

I want to be an actor! I go to acting school. At my new school, my teacher says I'm too quiet. She says I ¹ ___must___ talk more.

Sometimes we play a game. You throw a ball to a friend. They catch it and do something funny. Then they throw it to you and you do something funnier. But I can't catch the ball and my friends laugh at me.

I'm bad at acting.

Marina

Dear Marina,

You ² _____ worry! It's really difficult to start a new school, but you ³ _____ be quiet and shy. You must be more talkative.

When you play the game don't catch the ball. Drop it and do something funny. It's good to make your friends laugh. Or you ⁴ _____ learn to catch the ball and do something sporty. Or do both! An actor ⁵ _____ learn to do many things.

You must be hardworking and you ⁶ _____ learn to act! Then you can have lots of fun.

Jill

13 Look at activity 12. Read and match.

1 Marina's teacher says she's quiet. `b`
2 Marina says she can't catch the ball. ☐
3 Marina says her friends laugh at her. ☐
4 Marina says she's bad at acting. ☐

a Jill says it's good to be funny.
b Jill says she mustn't be shy.
c Jill says she must drop the ball to be funny or learn to catch it.
d Jill says she must be hardworking and learn to act.

14 **(TIP)** How to use *say/says*.

My teacher: You must be hardworking!

My teacher says I must be hardworking.

My parents: You mustn't be noisy.

My parents say I mustn't be noisy.

Read Marina's letter again and circle the things her teacher says.

Skills: *Writing*

15 Read and tick three problems you want to help with.

Dear (your name) _____ ,

I like my new sports school, but I'm not very good at sport.

I want to be a basketball player. My teacher says ...

☐ I can't catch/throw a ball.   ☐ I don't play every day.

☐ I'm not sporty.   ☐ I don't work hard.

☐ I'm noisy in the classroom.   ☐ My friend is sportier than me.

Please help,

Jim

16 Write the three problems you ticked in activity 15. Then make notes about help you can give.

1:	2:	3:

17 Write a help letter to Jim.

Dear Jim,

(your name)

Where are the places on the map?

1 Look and complete the sentences.

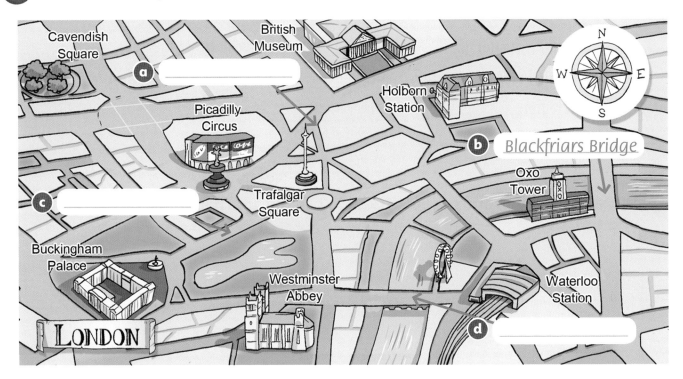

1 The _British Museum_ is in the north of the map.
2 South of Trafalgar Square is _____ .
3 You can see The Oxo Tower in the _____ of the map.
4 In the northwest of the map there's _____ Square.
5 Buckingham Palace is to the _____ of Westminster Abbey.

2 Read and write the places in activity 1. Use the words in the box.

~~Blackfriars Bridge~~   Monmouth Street   The Mall   Westminster Bridge

1 Blackfriars Bridge is to the east of the Oxo Tower.
2 Monmouth Street is to the south of the British museum and to the north of Trafalgar Square.
3 The Mall is to the southwest of Trafalgar Square.
4 Westminster Bridge is to the west of Waterloo Station and to the southeast of Trafalgar Square.

Evaluation

1 Read and correct the sentences.

1 You ~~must~~ run in the house.

_____ *mustn't* _____

2 We mustn't listen to our teachers.

_____

3 Tell me some paper, please.

_____

4 Read me my mobile phone, please.

_____

5 We mustn't be hardworking in class.

_____

6 Pass us the answer, please.

_____

2 (My World) Write sentences about you.

Write a rule for something you *must* do in school.

1 *I must* _____

Write a rule for something you *mustn't* do in school.

2 _____

Write an instruction for a friend.

3 _____

3 Complete the sentences about this unit.

✔ = I can …   ✗ = I can't …

☐ 1 … use words like *skipping*, *texting*, *helping*.

☐ 2 … talk about things we *must* and *mustn't* do.

☐ 3 … ask people to do things.

☐ 4 … be kind to animals.

☐ 5 … design and write about an unusual school and its rules.

6 The part of this unit I must practise is _____ .

Review Units 1 and 2

1 Read and complete the sentences. Use the words in the box.

> artistic   birthday   born   Brazil   clever   cry
> December   ~~funny~~   laugh   shout   sporty   throw

1 My best friend is very _____funny_____ . She tells jokes. Her jokes make me _____ .

2 We mustn't _____ or be noisy. We mustn't make the baby _____ .

3 Will's _____ is on the 16th of _____ .

4 My younger brother is very _____ . He plays basketball. He can _____ the ball very far.

5 The new student is from _____ . But she was _____ in Spain.

6 My older sister is _____ . She paints and makes films. Her films always have a _____ story.

2 Look and complete the sentences.

1 I'm _more hardworking than_ my brother. (hardworking)

2 Your cat _____ your dog. (naughty)

3 _____ , John or his sister? (tall)

4 We _____ drop litter on the ground. (mustn't/must)

3 **Read and complete the sentences.**

My name is Sam. There are three boys in my family. I was born on June 5th, 2006. I have two brothers. My brother Zack was born on May 4th, 2005. My other brother, Aiden, was born on July 6th, 2007.

Zack is tall and artistic. He's quiet and shy. He makes films. Aiden is short. He's noisy and sporty. He plays football. I'm not short or tall. I'm friendly and talkative. I like playing video games on my mobile phone.

old/young	1 Zack is ____older____ than me.	
	2 Aiden is _____ than me.	
tall/short	3 Zack is _____ than me.	
	4 Aiden is _____ than me.	
noisy/quiet	5 I'm _____ than Aiden.	
	6 I'm _____ than Zack.	

4 (Think) **Who is Sam's mum talking to? Look at activity 3 and write the names and the words.**

1 **Mum:** ____Aiden____ ! You _____ kick the ball in the house.

_____ me the ball, please.

2 **Mum:** _____ ! You _____ use your mobile phone during dinner.

3 **Mum:** _____ , _____ me your film, please. I really want to watch it.

5 (My World) **Answer the questions about you.**

1 How many sisters or brothers have you got? How are you different from them?

I have _____

_____

2 What things are you good at?

_____

_____

3 What are the rules in your home? Use *must* and *mustn't*.

_____

_____

3 Under the sea

1 **Look and write the words.**

 1

 2

 3

 4

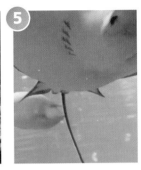 5

_____ crab _____   _____   _____   _____   _____

2 **Look, read and write the words.**

1 It's got eight legs. It likes hiding in rocks. _____ octopus _____

2 It's got five legs. It can be many different colours. _____

3 It's a big fish. It's got many sharp teeth. It's very dangerous!

_____

4 It's very big. It's very heavy too. It's not a fish. _____

5 It's got a shell. It's good at swimming.

_____

3 **Complete the table with the words in the box.**

Which sea animals have got … ?		
legs	**a shell**	**a long tail**
crab	_crab_	_____
_____	_____	_____
_____	_____	_____
_____	_____	_____

crab
octopus
starfish
stingray
turtle
shark

My picture dictionary → Go to page 87: Write the new words.

4 **Read and complete the table.**

dangerous	more dangerous	_the most dangerous_
heavy	heavier	
light	lighter	
intelligent	more intelligent	
strong	stronger	
weak	weaker	

5 **Complete the sentences. Use the words in brackets.**

1 Stingrays aren't ___the most dangerous___ sea animals. (dangerous)

2 Blue whales are _____ whales. (heavy)

3 Seals aren't _____ sea animals. (weak)

4 Whale sharks are _____ sharks. (strong)

5 Turtles aren't _____ sea animals. (light)

6 Dolphins are _____ sea animals. (intelligent)

6 **Look and complete the sentences.**

| heavy/light | fast/slow | dangerous/intelligent |

1 The crab is __the__
   lightest .

2 The seal is _____
   _____ .

3 The jellyfish is _____
   _____ .

4 The dolphin is _____

5 The dolphin is _____
   _____ .

6 The shark is _____
   _____ .

7 **Read and complete. Use the words in the box.**

> heavy̶   intelligent   fast   slow   tall   small

Elephants are ¹_____the heaviest_____ land animals. An elephant can weigh 7,000 kilograms.

Elephants can be tall too. But giraffes are ²_____ land animals. Giraffes

can be 5.5 metres high. What about small land animals? Do you think a mouse or

a bat is the smallest? ³_____ animals are bats. Bumblebee bats are only

30 mm long.⁴_____ land animals can run up to 120 kilometres per hour.

They are large cats called cheetahs and they live in Africa. ⁵_____ land

animals are tortoises. They move at 0.27 kilometers per hour. Which land animals are

⁶_____ ? Humans of course, but chimpanzees are very intelligent too.

8 (Think) **Read and number the pictures.**

elephant

chimpanzee

bumblebee bat

cheetah

1

1   It's not the strongest or the heaviest. It's not the smallest and it's not the most intelligent. It's the fastest.
2   It's not the tallest or the fastest. It's not the most intelligent. It's the smallest.
3   It's not the smallest, or the most intelligent. It's not the fastest. It's the strongest and the heaviest.
4   It's not the strongest or heaviest. It's not the fastest and it's not the smallest. It's very intelligent.

9 (My World) **Complete the questions and answers. Use the words in the box.**

> beautiful̶   friendly   interesting   dangerous

1   I think _____ are _____the most beautiful_____ sea animals.
2   I think _____ are _____ land animals.
3   Which sea animal is _____ ?
    I think _____ .
4   _____ animal is _____ ?
    I think _____ .

Read the story again. Match and then number.

	Capu finds _____	**a** to cut the net.
1	Jack, Ruby, and Sofia are by _b_	**b** the sea.
	Jack uses the shell _____	**c** is very friendly.
	The baby dolphin swims _____	**d** a baby dolphin. It needs help.
	The dolphin's pod _____	**e** to its pod.
	They see _____	**f** the biggest shell.

11 **Read and complete. Use the words in the box.**

> help   pleasure   pod   rubbish   ~~Africa~~   thank you

Jack, Ruby and Sofia are in ¹_____Africa_____ by the Indian Ocean. It's very beautiful.
The children see something in the water. At first, it looks like ²_____ . But it's
a baby dolphin.

They find shells and they use them to ³_____ the dolphin. The dolphin
swims with its ⁴_____ . The dolphin pod says ⁵_____ . It was
a ⁶_____ for the children to help.

12   **What can you do to show the value:
keep our seas and oceans clean?**

1 Don't throw bottles in the _____sea_____ .

2 Don't make a _____ .

3 Tidy up after a _____ .

4 Don't drop _____ .

Story   Value   **33**

Skills: *Reading*

13 Read Sara's blog and circle the correct words.

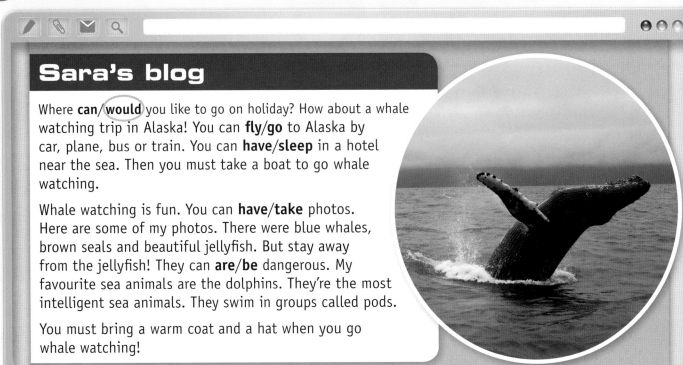

Sara's blog

Where **can**/**would** you like to go on holiday? How about a whale watching trip in Alaska! You can **fly**/**go** to Alaska by car, plane, bus or train. You can **have**/**sleep** in a hotel near the sea. Then you must take a boat to go whale watching.

Whale watching is fun. You can **have**/**take** photos. Here are some of my photos. There were blue whales, brown seals and beautiful jellyfish. But stay away from the jellyfish! They can **are**/**be** dangerous. My favourite sea animals are the dolphins. They're the most intelligent sea animals. They swim in groups called pods.

You must bring a warm coat and a hat when you go whale watching!

14 Look at activity 13. Read and write *true* or *false*.

1 You can go to Alaska by underground.   *false*

2 You must take a boat to go whale watching.

3 Sara's got photos of blue starfish,
   brown crabs and a friendly jellyfish.

4 Sara's favourite sea animals are octopuses.

5 You must bring warm clothes when you go whale watching.

15 **(TIP)** **How to use commas** (,).

When talking about two things, you don't need a comma:
I saw a dolphin and a whale.
When talking about more than two things, you do need a comma:
I saw a dolphin, a whale, a shark, a seal <u>and</u> a starfish.
Write *and* before the last thing:
We took a plane, a bus <u>and</u> a train.

Read Sara's blog again and:
1 circle the commas.
2 <u>underline</u> the sentence with two things that don't need a comma.

Skills: *Writing*

16   **Make notes about a place you want to go to.**

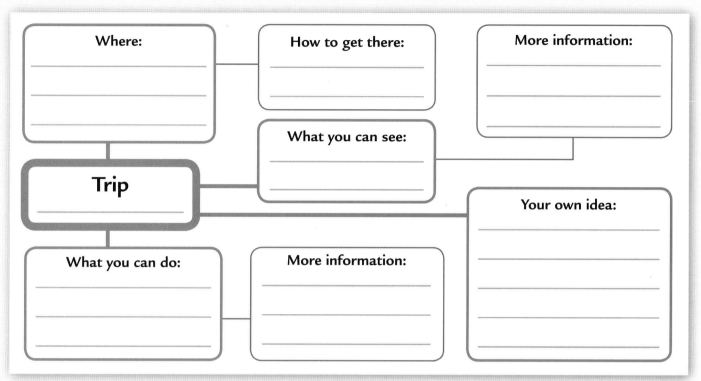

Where:
_____
_____
_____

How to get there:
_____
_____

More information:
_____
_____
_____

What you can see:
_____
_____

Trip
_____

Your own idea:
_____
_____
_____
_____

What you can do:
_____
_____
_____

More information:
_____
_____
_____

17 **Write a blog and draw a picture.**

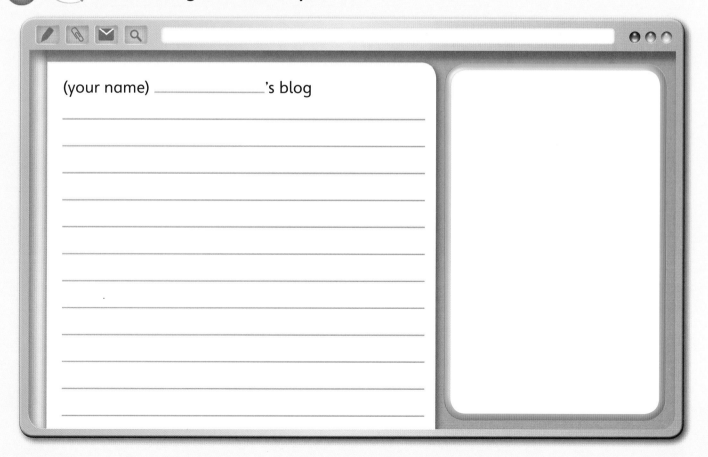

(your name) _____'s blog

What is an underwater food chain?

1 **Read and complete the sentences.**

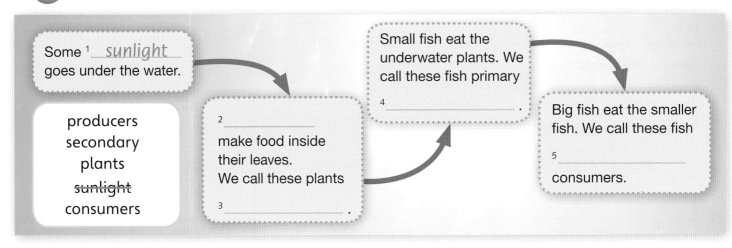

Some ¹ _sunlight_ goes under the water.

producers
secondary
plants
~~sunlight~~
consumers

² _____
make food inside their leaves.
We call these plants
³ _____ .

Small fish eat the underwater plants. We call these fish primary
⁴ _____ .

Big fish eat the smaller fish. We call these fish
⁵ _____
consumers.

2 **Look, read and number the pictures.**

1 sunlight   **2** producer   **3** primary consumer   **4** secondary consumer

grass   snake   sun `1`   snail

butterfly   flowers   bird   sun

3 **Look at activity 2. Write the words.**

1 Snakes eat snails. Snakes are _secondary consumers_ .

2 Sunlight helps flowers to make food. Flowers are _____ .

3 Snails eat grass. Snails are _____ .

4 Flowers and grass need _____ to make food.

Evaluation

1 **Read and complete.**

My name is Tina I want to go scuba diving in the ocean. I would like to swim with ¹ <u>turtles</u> . They are good at swimming. And they are the oldest sea animals too.

I wouldn't want to see any dangerous ² _____ . They've got a lot of teeth! And I would swim away from the most dangerous sea animals, box ³ _____ .

I would like to see ⁴ _____ . They like to play games. ⁵ _____ are the biggest sea animals. And I think whales are the most beautiful sea animals.

I would like to keep our oceans clean for all of the sea animals.

2 **Look at activity 1. Put the words in order and write the answers.**

1   are / oldest / sea animals? / Which / the
<u>Which are the oldest sea animals</u>?   <u>turtles</u>

2   the / Which / most / sea animals? / are / dangerous

3   the / biggest / sea animals? / are / Which

4   think / most / beautiful / are the / sea animals? / Which / does / Tina

3 **Complete the sentences about this unit.**

✓ = I can …   ✗ = I can't …

   1 … name ten sea animals.
   2 … talk about animals using -est and the most.
   3 … ask and answer questions using Which … ? and the most.
   4 … keep our seas and oceans clean.
   5 … plan and talk about a weekend trip using I'd like to.
6   The part of this unit I found the most interesting is _____ .

4 Gadgets

1 Write the words.

1 m e g a s   n e s c o o l
  games console

2 b a l e t t
  _____

3 d o i v e   m a r e c a
  _____

4 s h e d o n h a p e
  _____

5 l i g t a d i   c a r e a m
  _____

6 P4M   r y l e p a
  _____

2 Think Read and complete the sentences.

1 He likes taking photos. He hasn't got a camera.
  He uses his _smartphone_ .

2 She likes playing games. She uses her
  _____ with the television.

3 He likes reading books. He doesn't have
  a tablet. He uses an _____ .

4 She does her homework on her _____ . It's bigger than her tablet and
  she takes it to the library.

5 He watches films on the _____ . It's bigger than his laptop.

3 Think Read and circle the odd ones out.

1 You can listen to music on … .
  a a laptop **b** a smartphone **c** an MP4 player **d** (a video camera)

2 You can play games on … .
  a a digital camera **b** a games console **c** a tablet **d** a laptop

3 You can read books on … .
  a a tablet **b** headphones **c** an e-reader **d** a smartphone

4 You can use the internet on … .
  a a tablet **b** a laptop **c** a video camera **d** a smartphone

My picture dictionary → Go to page 88: Write the new words.

4 Complete the sentences about yesterday with words in the box.

listen to   ~~play~~   study   use   ~~visit~~   watch

1

I _____visited_____ my grandmother.

2

We _didn't play_ tennis.

3

He _____ a smartphone to take photos.

4

They _____ television in the evening.

5

She _____ music with her headphones.

6

You _____ English in the garden.

5 Read and correct the sentences.

1 They ~~visited~~ a film last night before bed.   _____watched_____

2 I didn't play for my science test yesterday evening.   _____

3 I listened to films on my tablet last weekend.   _____

4 We studied games on our smartphones this morning before school. _____

5 He didn't watch to music on his MP4 player last night. _____

6 She used her grandmother last Saturday.   _____

6 **My World** Write about last week. Use the words in the box and your own ideas.

1 Last week, I _____ _studied English._

2 Last week, I didn't _____

3 _____

4 _____

use   ~~study~~
watch   play

7 Read and complete the questions and answers.

Dear Sheila,

Thank you for the birthday present! It's lovely! I'm sorry you missed my birthday party last Saturday. It was fun. We played on my new games console. I walked my dog in the park on Sunday.

How is your trip to Paris? Tell me about it! Send photos!

Take care, Rian

Dear Rian,

I'm glad you like the hat. Sorry I missed your party. Paris is wonderful. I visited my cousins on Saturday. They don't speak English, but we played on a games console. On Sunday, we looked at paintings in the Louvre Museum and shopped on a street called the Champs-Élysées.

See you soon, Sheila

1 What _____*did*_____ Rian _____*do*_____ at her party?

She _*played on a games console*_ .

2 What _____ Rian _____ last Sunday?

She _____ in the park.

3 What _____ Sheila _____ with her cousins last Saturday?

They _____ .

4 _____ Sheila _____ last Sunday?

She _____ at paintings in the Louvre Museum and _____ on a street called the Champs-Élysées.

8 (My World) Complete the questions and answers. Use your own information.

1 What did you do last night? _Last night, I watched TV._

2 What didn't you do last night? _____

3 What did you do last Saturday? _____

4 What did you do yesterday after school? _____

9 **Read the story again and complete the sentences. Then number.**

a   They find a _____ from 1950.

b   The explorers think the _____ is a wonderful gadget.

c   They must help the _____ .

1 d   The children are in _Antarctica_ . It's cold.

e   Then they use the tablet to ask for _____ .

~~Antarctica~~
diary
tablet
help
explorers

10 **Read and match.**

1   There aren't any _b_

2   The explorers are very _____

3   The children use blankets _____

4   A helicopter takes _____

5   The explorers say 'thanks' _____

a   cold and they need help.

b   trees in Antarctica.

c   to the children.

d   to help the explorers.

e   the explorers to hospital.

11 **Write the sentences. Then tick the ones that show the value: use technology wisely.**

1   laptop / to / can / You / a / use / do homework.

You can use a laptop to do homework.   ✓

2   study English. / a tablet / use / You / can / to

_____

3   play / can / in / You / a / games console / on / class.

_____

4   to ask / use / mobile phone / You / for help. / a / can

_____

Story   Value   **41**

Skills: *Reading*

12 Read Ben's report and circle the correct answers.

Inventions, by Ben

1

GRIDpad tablet

2

Television

Samsung invented the first tablet in 1989. They called it the GRIDpad. It was bigger and heavier than the tablets we have today. You used a pen with it!

Then, Jeff Hawkins invented a smaller tablet called the Palm Pilot in 1996. It used the GRIDpad's pen. The Palm Pilot was really cool!

John Logie Baird didn't invent the television. Many people worked together to invent the television. But John Logie Baird showed the first television pictures to people. The first television pictures were black and white. John Logie Baird showed the first colour pictures to people on July 3, 1928. The first television used a telephone to send pictures!

1 Which gadget was invented in 1989?
   a the laptop   b the television   c (the tablet)
2 How was the first tablet different from today's tablets?
   a It was bigger and heavier.   b It was smaller and lighter.
   c It was bigger and lighter.
3 Who showed the first television pictures to people?
   a Jeff Hawkins   b John Logie Baird   c many people
4 What did people see on July 3, 1928?
   a pictures on black and white television   b pictures on colour television
   c pictures on a tablet
5 Which gadget was invented first?
   a the Palm Pilot   b the television   c the GRIDpad

13 **TIP** **How to use full stops ()and exclamation marks ().**
Usually you use a full stop to end a sentence: *It's an old laptop.*

You can use an exclamation mark when you want to: shout – *Hey! Wow!*
make sentences stronger and more exciting – *It's great! Thanks!*

Read Ben's report again and circle the exclamation marks.

Skills: *Writing*

14 Find out about a gadget or other invention. Make notes about it.

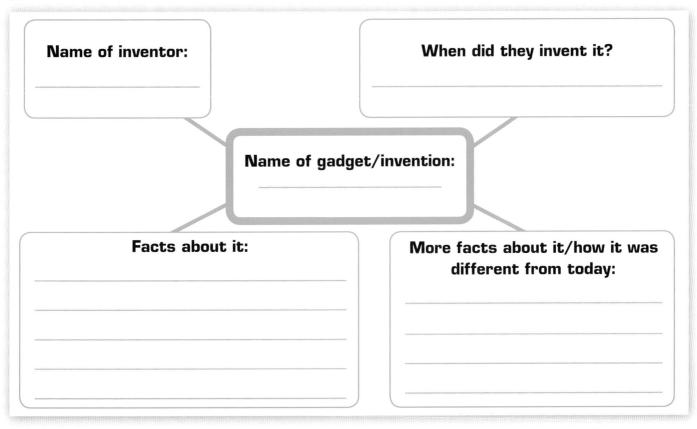

Name of inventor:

_____

When did they invent it?

_____

Name of gadget/invention:

_____

Facts about it:

_____
_____
_____
_____
_____

More facts about it/how it was different from today:

_____
_____
_____
_____

15 Write a report about the gadget or invention.

Title: _____

_____
_____
_____
_____
_____
_____
_____
_____
_____
_____

How do we read a line graph?

1 How many computer games did the class buy last year?
Draw the data on the line graph.

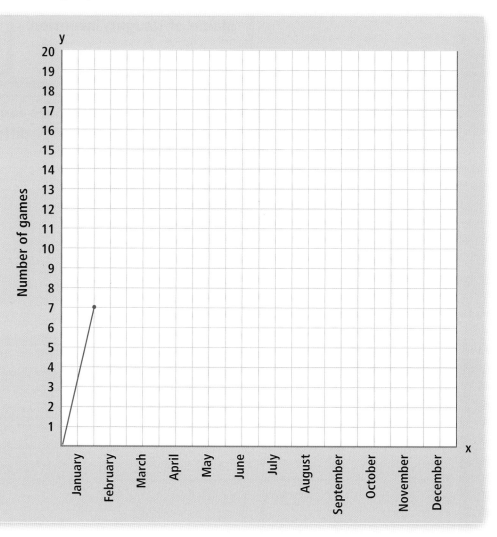

Month	Number of computer games
January	7
February	3
March	10
April	12
May	9
June	6
July	16
August	18
September	4
October	7
November	5
December	20

2 Look at activity 1. Answer the questions.

1 What data is on the x-axis?   _the months_

2 What data is on the y-axis?   _____

3 Which month shows the peak for buying computer games?   _____

4 When is the biggest rise in buying computer games?   _____

5 When is the biggest fall in buying computer games?   _____

Evaluation

1 **Read the conversation and correct the eight mistakes.**

Dana: What do you do last weekend, Brice?

Brice: I play on my game console. Then I watch a football game on television. What did you do?

Dana: I study on my e-reader. Then I listen to music on my new MP4 player. What did you do, Helen?

Helen: I use my smartphone to make a video.

Dana: Can we watch it?

Helen: Sure. Here it is. I use my laptop to add music to the video.

Dana: That's great!

Brice: Tom, what did you do last weekend?

Dana: Hey! Look! Is that Tom in the video?

Tom: Yes, that's me. I help Helen make her video!

1 _____did_____   2 _____   3 _____   4 _____

5 _____   6 _____   7 _____   8 _____

2 **Look at activity 1. Complete the questions and answers.**

1 What ___did___ Brice ___do___ last weekend?

He _played on his games console_ and _watched a football game on television_ .

2 What _____ Dana _____ last weekend?

She _____ . Then she _____ .

3 Which gadgets _____ Helen use last weekend?

She used her _____ and her _____ to make a video.

4 What _____ Tom _____ last weekend? He _____ .

3 **Complete the sentences about this unit.**

✓ = I can …   ✗ = I can't …

☐ 1 … name ten gadgets.

☐ 2 … say what I did last weekend using *watched*, *listened*, *played*, *used*, *visited* and *studied*.

☐ 3 … ask and answer questions using *What did you do … ?*

☐ 4 … use technology wisely.

☐ 5 … think and write about my favourite gadget.

6 The part of this unit I found the most useful is _____ .

Review Units 3 and 4

1 Look and complete the word puzzle.

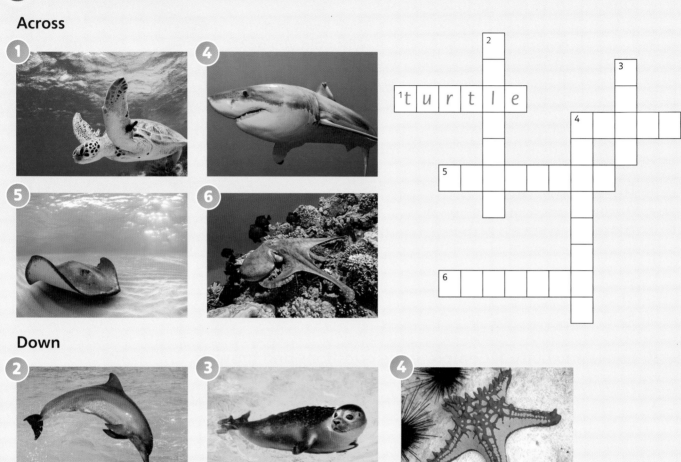

Across

1 ● [turtle image]
4 ● [shark image]
5 ● [stingray image]
6 ● [octopus image]

Crossword grid:
1 ¹t u r t l e

Down

2 ● [dolphin image]
3 ● [seal image]
4 ● [starfish image]

2 Read and complete the sentences.

1 You wear ___headphones___ on your head to listen to music.

2 A _____ is a computer. It's smaller than a laptop and bigger than a smartphone.

3 You keep your music on an _____ . You can't make phone calls or watch films on it. But you can use it to listen to music.

4 I like to read books on my _____ . I can only use it to read books.

5 My _____ is smaller than my laptop and it does more things. I can use it as an MP4 player, as a video camera and to talk to my friends!

6 My favourite technology is my _____ . I really like video games.

3 **Look and complete the questions and answers. Then match.**

1 What ___did___ ___you___ ___do___ in the park last weekend? [c]

2 _____ sea animal is the most intelligent? [ ]

3 _____ bird is the strongest? [ ]

4 What _____ you watch on television last night? [ ]

a The dolphin is the _____ intelligent.

b I _____ a programme about sharks on television.

c I ___played___ football with my friends.

d The eagle is the _____ bird.

4 (Think) **Read and complete the sentences.**

Abby watched a TV programme about the heaviest sea animal last night.
Alan and Tina played a game about the strongest sea animal on their smartphones.
Tom did a quiz on his tablet last night. He learned about the most dangerous sea animal.
Rose used her laptop last night. She looked at pictures of the most dangerous fish.

1 Rose ___didn't___ ___play___ on her smartphone. She ___looked___ ___at___ ___pictures___ of ___sharks___ .

2 _____ and _____ played a game on their _____ .

3 _____ , _____ , and _____ looked at whales last night.
   But they _____ _____ the same gadgets.

4 Tom _____ about box _____ .

5 Abby didn't use a laptop or smartphone last night. She _____ television.

5 (My World) **Answer the questions about you.**

1 What are your favourite sea animals? _My favourite sea animals are_ _____

2 What did you do last weekend? _____

3 What didn't you do last weekend? _____

4 Which gadget is your favourite? _____

5 The natural world

1 Read and circle the correct words.

1 You can climb a … . It's tall.
  a (mountain)　**b** forest　　**c** jungle

2 A … is like a mountain. It's very hot and dangerous.
  a mountain　**b** island　　**c** volcano

3 You find this land in an ocean or a lake. You can go to an … by boat.
  a island　　**b** cave　　**c** lake

4 A … is smaller than the sea. People go sailing on it.
  a lake　　**b** island　　**c** river

5 A … is water that moves across land. The Amazon is the name of one.
  a desert　　**b** lake　　**c** river

6 The Amazon is also the name of a … . It's hot and has a lot of trees.
  a mountain　**b** jungle　　**c** desert

7 There are many trees in a … . It can be cold or hot.
  a lake　　**b** volcano　　**c** forest

8 It's very hot and there is sand in the … .
  a volcano　**b** desert　　**c** waterfall

9 A … is under the ground or in a mountain. Bats sometimes live in it.
  a desert　　**b** waterfall　**c** cave

10 Water that falls from a mountain or higher land is a … .
  a waterfall　**b** lake　　**c** island

2 Write the sentences.

1 (island / small / ocean)
  An island is smaller than an ocean.

2 (mountain / tall / tree)

3 (forest / cool / jungle)
  Usually,

4 (desert / dry / jungle)

My picture dictionary Go to page 89: Write the new words.

3 Read Dave's and Amber's holiday lists. Correct the mistakes in the sentences.

Dave's holiday

	swim in the lake
✓	catch fish
✓	go to the forest
	see a deer
✓	eat fish
	eat pizza
✓	drink tea

Amber's holiday

✓	go skiing
	go snowboarding
✓	drink tea
✓	eat chocolate
	eat pizza
✓	have a party
✓	swim at the hotel

1 Dave and Amber ~~drink~~ tea on their holidays. _____drank_____

2 Dave don't swim in a lake on his holiday. _____

Amber swim at the hotel. _____

3 Dave eat fish. Amber eat chocolate. _____ _____

4 Amber don't go snowboarding. She go skiing. _____ _____

5 Dave don't have a party. Amber don't go to the forest. _____ _____

4 Look at activity 3. Read and complete the answers.

1 Where did Dave go?   Dave _went to the forest_____ .

2 What didn't Dave see?   Dave _____ .

3 What did Dave catch?   He _____ .

4 What did Amber have?   Amber _____ .

5 What didn't Amber or Dave eat?   They _____ .

5 **My World** Answer the questions about you.

1 Where did you go on your favourite holiday?

_On my favourite holiday, I went to_____

2 What did you do on your favourite holiday?

_____

3 What didn't you do on your favourite holiday?

_____

4 What did you eat on your favourite holiday?

_____

6 (Think) **Complete the questions and answers.**

Mum: ¹___Did___ you ²___go___ on a trip this afternoon?

Mel: Yes, I ³___did___ .
My class ⁴_____ on a trip.

Mum: ⁵_____ you swim in a lake?

Mel: No, I ⁶_____ .

Mum: ⁷_____ you see a painting?

Mel: No, I ⁸_____ . I saw a cow.

Mum: A cow? ⁹_____ you ¹⁰_____ horses?

Mel: Yes, I ¹¹_____ . I saw horses, cows and bees.

Mum: That's nice. ¹²_____ you ¹³_____ milk?

Mel: Yes, I ¹⁴_____ . I drank milk from the cows. I ate apples from the trees too.

Mum: Hmm, apples, cows … I know!
¹⁵_____ you visit a ¹⁶_____ ?

Mel: Yes, I did!

7 (My World) **Complete the questions and answers about you.**

1 ___Did___ you ___drink___ coffee yesterday?

_____

2 _____ your family _____ a museum yesterday?

_____

3 _____ your friend _____ to school yesterday?

_____

4 _____ your friend _____ in a lake yesterday?

_____

8 (Think) **Read the story again. Then put the words in order and number.**

a can't / he / Jack / thinks / act. /

[ ] _____

b doesn't / bats. / Sofia / like

[ ] _____

c the / The / director / thanks / children.

[ ] _____

d a / are / children / cave. / in / The

[1] *The children are in a cave.*

e The / children / director / the / needs / to help.

[ ] _____

9 **Read and circle the correct words.**

1 Ruby doesn't like … .
  a acting   b bats   c (the dark)

2 There are … in the cave.
  a actors   b bats   c a director

3 They can help because the director needs … .
  a doesn't worry   b actors   c is in the United States

4 Jack worries about … .
  a acting   b dogs   c the dark

5 Hollywood is … .
  a a movie   b where they take Capu   c in the United States

10 (My World) **Write the sentences. Then tick the ones that show the value: encourage your friends.**

1 can / You / it! / do
  You can do it! [✓]

2 not / good at / You're / sport!
  _____ [ ]

3 actor! / a / You're / great
  _____ [ ]

4 We / can / you! / help
  _____ [ ]

5 cooking! / You / good at / aren't
  _____ [ ]

Skills: *Reading*

11 Read the holiday reviews. Change the <u>underlined</u> words to say what happened. Then match.

HOLIDAY HIKES REVIEWS

1 Amazon river jungle trip, by Amy

I ¹<u>go</u> on the Amazon River jungle trip in July. That was a good time to go because it wasn't rainy. I ²<u>go</u> on a boat trip down the long river. I didn't swim in the river because I ³<u>see</u> a big snake in the water. We ⁴<u>eat</u> lots of delicious bananas on this trip. My favourite part of the trip? I ⁵<u>see</u> a monkey and a jaguar!

2 Grand canyon horse ride, by Jim

I ⁶<u>see</u> so many things in the Grand Canyon! It's not just rocks and sand. Our guide pointed to many green lizards, pretty birds, and beautiful flowers! We ⁷<u>go</u> on horses. But sometimes the naughty horses wouldn't walk! We ⁸<u>eat</u> biscuits and ⁹<u>drink</u> water. At night, it was very dark. We ¹⁰<u>see</u> so many stars. It was beautiful.

1 _went_   4 _____   7 _____   10 _____

2 _____   5 _____   8 _____

3 _____   6 _____   9 _____

12 Look at activity 11. Answer the questions.

1 Does it rain in July in the Amazon? _No, it doesn't._

2 What was Amy's favourite part of her trip? _____

3 What animals can you see in the Grand Canyon? _____

4 What were the horses like? _____

13 **(TIP)** **How to describe things.**

Use lots of different words to make your reviews more interesting:

I went down a *long* river.

I saw *green* lizards, *pretty* birds and *beautiful* flowers.

Read the holiday reviews again and:

1 circle three examples of words that describe things in Amy's review.

2 circle five examples of words that describe things in Jim's review.

Skills: *Writing*

14 **Make notes about a place you visited. Use words to describe things.**

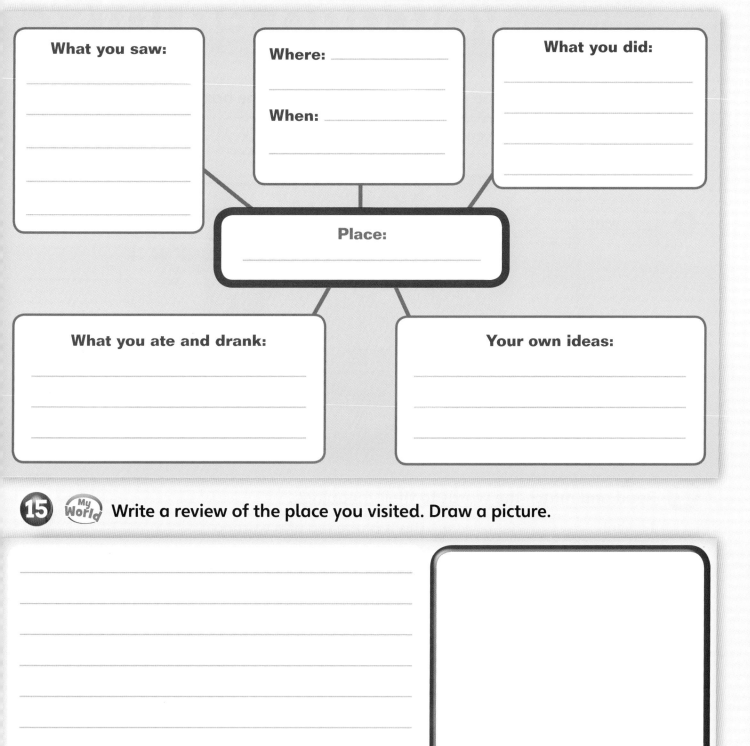

What you saw:

_____
_____
_____
_____

Where: _____

_____

When: _____

_____

What you did:

_____
_____
_____
_____

Place:

_____

What you ate and drank:

_____
_____
_____

Your own ideas:

_____
_____
_____

15 **Write a review of the place you visited. Draw a picture.**

What happens when a volcano erupts?

1 Look and complete the picture with the words in the box.

> ~~vent~~   crater   lava   ash   rock

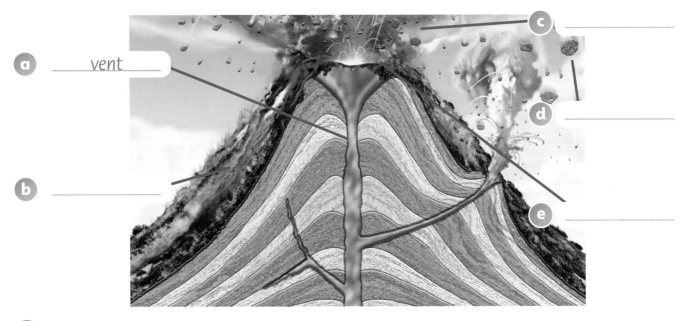

a vent

b _____

c _____

d _____

e _____

2 Read and match the words to their meanings.

1	vent	c	a This is at the top of a volcano.
2	crater		b Hot lava can stop these growing.
3	lava		c This is inside a volcano. Very hot material comes up it.
4	ash and rocks		d This very hot material comes from inside the volcano.
5	plants		e These fly into the air above the erupting volcano.

3 Read and complete the sentences. Then number.

[ ] a The lava cools and turns to _____ .

[ ] b Lava covers the _____ and they stop growing.

[1] c You can see _____rocks_____ and _____ in the air.

[ ] d _____ runs down the sides of the volcano.

> plants
> ash
> rock
> ~~rocks~~
> lava

Evaluation

1 **Complete the questions and answers.**

1 **Erin:** I ¹_____went_____ somewhere interesting this weekend.

Jack: ²_____Did_____ you ³_____see_____ any birds?

Erin: No, I didn't, but I ⁴_____ bats!

Jack: Let me guess. Was it dark?

Erin: Yes!

Jack: You ⁵_____ to a ⁶_____ .

2 **Dan:** Mike, guess where I ⁷_____ on holiday!

Mike: ⁸_____ you ⁹_____ lots of trees?

Dan: Yes, we ¹⁰_____ , but we didn't climb them.

Mike: ¹¹_____ you ¹²_____ hot chocolate?

Dan: Yes, we ¹³_____ .

Mike: ¹⁴_____ you ¹⁵_____ snowboarding or skiing?

Dan: Yes, we ¹⁶_____ .

Mike: I know! You ¹⁷_____ to the ¹⁸_____ !

2 **Look at activity 1. Answer the questions.**

1 Did Erin see any birds on holiday?   _No, she didn't._

2 Did Erin go to a dark place?   _____

3 Did Dan climb any trees?   _____

4 Did Dan drink hot chocolate?   _____

3 **Complete the sentences about this unit.**

✓ = I can …   ✗ = I can't …

☐ 1 … name ten places in the natural world.

☐ 2 … say what I did in my holiday using *had*, *went*, *saw*, *swam*, *ate*, *drank* and *caught*.

☐ 3 … ask and answer *yes* and *no* questions using *Did you … ?*

☐ 4 … encourage my friends.

☐ 5 … think and write about my favourite holiday.

6 The part of this unit I enjoyed was _____ .

6 Helping at home

1 Read and complete the sentences.

Every morning, I get up.
Then I _make my bed_ .

We _____
every week.

Every day, my mum
_____ .

My sister usually
_____ .

Sometimes I help my mum
_____ .

I play football and then I
_____ .

2 Complete the table.

Things you do in the kitchen	Things you do in the bedroom	Things you do in many rooms
dry the dishes	_____	_____
_____	_____	_____

3 Think Circle the odd ones out.

1 Tidy the ... .
  a basement   b (football)   c living room   d desk
2 Dry ... .
  a your clothes b your hair   c a headache   d the dishes
3 Clean the ... .
  a boat   b car   c bike   d talkative
4 Sweep the ... .
  a floor   b garage   c stairs   d sunny

My picture dictionary ➔ Go to page 90: Write the new words.

4 **Read and circle the correct words.**

Hi Kayla,

Do you ¹**have to**/**don't have to** help at home? We do! First, my older sister ²**has to**/**doesn't have to** make breakfast. Then, I ³**have to**/**don't have to** wash the dishes and dry them. But I ⁴**have to**/**don't have to** sweep the floor. My sister has to do that.

And I'm happy I ⁵**have to**/**don't have to** put the rubbish out. My younger brother ⁶**has to**/**doesn't have to** do that.

Write back soon!

Your friend, Jackie

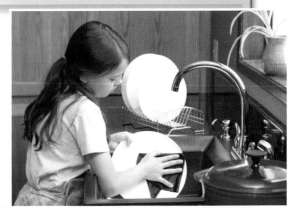

Hi Jackie,

You're busy! My parents do everything, so I usually ⁷**have to**/**don't have to** help at my house.

This week is different. I ⁸**have to**/**don't have to** help around my grandmother's house. I ⁹**have to**/**don't have to** wash clothes for her. Then, I ¹⁰**have to**/**don't have to** tidy the living room. I ¹¹**have to**/**don't have to** cook dinner for her. My brother does that.

What do you have to do this weekend? Can we go to the cinema?

Your friend, Kayla

5 **Look at activity 4. Write the questions and answers.**

1 (Jackie / make breakfast)

Does Jackie have to make breakfast?   _No, she doesn't._

2 (Jackie / wash and dry dishes)

_____   _____

3 (Jackie's sister / sweep the floor)

_____   _____

4 (Jackie / put the rubbish out)

_____   _____

5 (Kayla / tidy the living room / this week)

_____   _____

6 (Kayla's grandmother / cook dinner / this week)

_____   _____

6 **Put the words in order. Then match with the correct answers.**

1 you / have / Monday? / on / to / What / do / do
   <u>*What do you have to do on Monday?*</u> | b |

   a They have to wash the car.

2 What / on / John / do / have / to / Monday? / does
   _____ | |

   b I have to tidy my bedroom.

3 on / Tuesday? / do / have / does / Poppy / What / to
   _____ | |

   c Ethan does.

4 has / the / Who / on / wash / to / Tuesday? / car
   _____ | |

   d He has to put the rubbish out.

5 Tina and Rob / do / What / have / to / do / on / Tuesday?
   _____ | |

   e She has to clean the kitchen.

7 Think **Look at activity 6.**
Write the names in the table.

	Monday	Tuesday
clean the kitchen	Tina and Rob	
put the rubbish out		me
tidy my bedroom	*me*	John
wash the car	Poppy	

8 My World **Complete the questions and answers about you.**

1 What do you have to do on Monday?
   <u>*On Monday, I have to*</u> _____

2 What do you have to do in English class?
   _____

3 Who has to go to school?
   _____

4 What does your friend have to do tomorrow?
   _____

5 Who has to do homework?
   _____

9 Look, read and write *true* or *false*.

Picture 1

1	The children are helping the people.	_true_
2	Capu is watering the plants.	_____
3	Sophia is sweeping the stairs.	_____
4	Ruby is painting the palace.	_____

Picture 2

5	Capu wants to help the man.	_____
6	Capu can't find the key.	_____

10 Think Read the story again. Match and then number.

☐	Capu finds _____	**a**	the workers finish the palace.
☐	The workers have to _____	**b**	the key on the worker.
1	The children are at a palace _d_	**c**	finish the palace.
☐	The worker can't _____	**d**	in Ancient Egypt.
☐	The children help _____	**e**	find the key to the palace.

11 What can you do to show the value: help other people?

1 _You can dry the dishes._

2 _____

3 _____

4 _____

5 _____

Skills: *Reading*

 12 **Read and complete the postcards with *have to* or *don't have to*.**

Dear Alex,

I live at my grandpa's house now. He has lots of pets! We ¹ _____have to_____ wake up early every day. Then we feed the dogs, cats and fish. On Saturday, I ² _____ wash the rabbits. They are my favourite animals! We ³ _____ buy any fruit because grandpa grows it in his garden! Grandpa's fruit is really good! We ⁴ _____ help him in the garden after school.

Do you like living on a houseboat?

Write to me soon!
Lola

Dear Lola,

Thanks for your postcard! My family's houseboat is small! We ⁵ _____ be very tidy. We ⁶ _____ buy food often because we grow vegetables on the boat. We also share a garden on the land.

There is a bird's nest on the roof. We ⁷ _____ feed the birds because they eat fish from the river.

Come and visit and see the seals! They're always near the boat!
Alex

13 **Look at activity 12. Answer the questions.**

1 What does Lola do in the morning? _She feeds the dogs, cats and fish._

2 Who buys fruit more often? Lola or Alex? _____

3 What does Lola do after school? _____

4 What two animals can Alex see? _____

5 What does Alex want Lola to do? _____

 14 **(TIP) How to use apostrophes (').**

We use apostrophes to show that a person or thing has got something.

The family's car … = The car that the family has got.
The dog's toy. = The toy that the dog has got.

Read the letters again and circle the apostrophes that show that people or animals have got something.

Skills: *Writing*

15 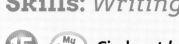 Circle *at home* or *at school*. Make notes about things you *have to / don't have to* do.

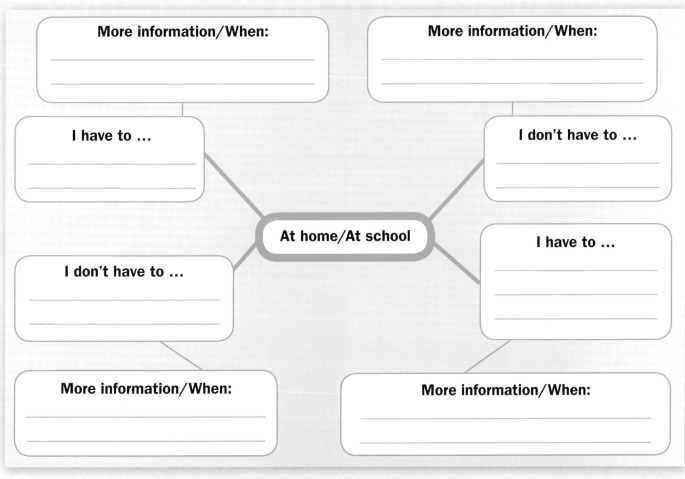

More information/When:
_____
_____

More information/When:
_____
_____

I have to …
_____
_____

I don't have to …
_____
_____

At home/At school

I don't have to …
_____
_____

I have to …
_____
_____
_____

More information/When:
_____
_____

More information/When:
_____
_____

16 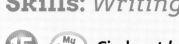 Write a postcard to a friend about what you *have to / don't have to* do.

Dear _____ ,
_____
_____
_____
_____
_____
_____
_____
_____

(your name) _____

What were castle homes like?

1 Look and complete the picture with the words in the box.

water   tower   ~~wall~~   hall   candle   fire

1 _wall_

2 _____

3 _____

4 _____

5 _____

6 _____

2 Read and complete.

In the middle ages, there was [1] _water_ around most castles. There were also big

strong [2]_____ . They had tall [3]_____ in them. Inside castles, families

had meals around a long, wooden [4]_____ in the hall. People used

[5]_____ to see at night. The castles had a [6]_____ for cooking food on

a big fire. Outside, there was a garden with fruit and [7]_____ to eat.

3 Imagine you go to a castle in the Middle Ages and meet a child there. Write
three questions for the child about life in the castle.

1 _Do you have to_ _____ ?

2 _____ ?

3 _____ ?

Evaluation

1 Look and write what they have to do.

1

I _have to make my bed._

2

Olivia _____

_____

_____

_____

3

Liam _____

_____

_____

4

Keira and Mia _____

_____

_____

2 (Think!) Put the words in order. Then look at activity 1 and match.

1 has / clean / Who / to / the / bathroom?
Who has to clean the bathroom? [c]

2 Liam / Does / to / have / bed? / make / his
_____ [ ]

3 Olivia / have / sweep / the / to / floor? / Does
_____ [ ]

4 do / do? / have / to / Kiera and Mia / What
_____ [ ]

5 Do / to / put / have / rubbish / the / out? / I
_____ [ ]

a Yes, she does.

b No. I don't.

c Liam does.

d Dry the dishes.

e No, he doesn't.

3 Complete the sentences about this unit.

✔ = I can …   ✗ = I can't …

[ ] **1** … name ten ways to help at home.

[ ] **2** … talk about things _I have to_ and _I don't have to_ do.

[ ] **3** … ask and answer questions using _What … ?_ and _Who … ?_

[ ] **4** … help other people.

[ ] **5** … design and talk about a home.

6 The part of this unit I have to practise is _____ .

Review Units 5 and 6

1 Look and write the words. Then find and circle.

1 island
2 _____
3 _____
4 _____
5 _____
6 _____
7 _____
8 _____
9 _____

L	A	K	E	E	N	G	Y	E
I	M	O	U	N	T	A	I	N
V	O	L	C	A	N	O	R	I
R	F	O	R	E	S	T	D	I
I	V	F	R	G	E	R	E	S
V	E	N	E	I	A	F	S	L
E	A	E	T	E	A	J	E	A
R	J	U	N	G	L	E	R	N
C	A	V	E	R	A	E	T	D

2 What did they do yesterday? Look and complete the sentences.

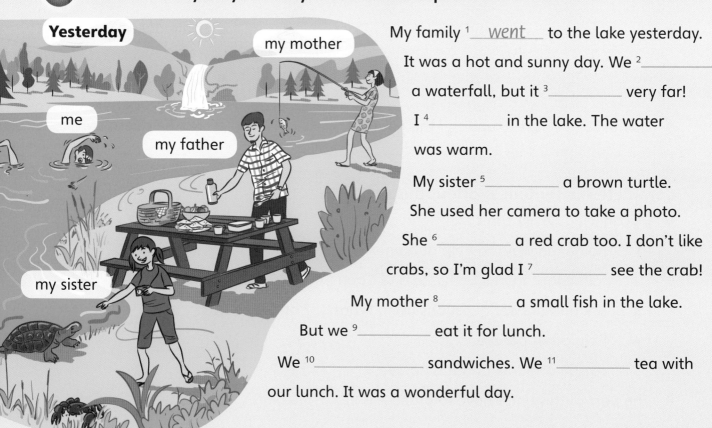

Yesterday

my mother

me

my father

my sister

My family ¹ __went__ to the lake yesterday.
It was a hot and sunny day. We ² _____
a waterfall, but it ³ _____ very far!
I ⁴ _____ in the lake. The water
was warm.

My sister ⁵ _____ a brown turtle.
She used her camera to take a photo.
She ⁶ _____ a red crab too. I don't like
crabs, so I'm glad I ⁷ _____ see the crab!
My mother ⁸ _____ a small fish in the lake.
But we ⁹ _____ eat it for lunch.
We ¹⁰ _____ sandwiches. We ¹¹ _____ tea with
our lunch. It was a wonderful day.

3 Read and complete the table.

My new school, by Jane

I went to my new school last month. It's a special school for Dance. I live at school now.
I visit my parents on weekends.
At my new school, I have to be hardworking. I have to dance every morning and afternoon!
I have to study at night. I'm very busy, but I love dancing.
At school, I don't have to wash my clothes or clean the kitchen, but I have to make my bed.
I never have to wash the dishes or put the rubbish out. It's great!

have to	don't have to
be hardworking	_____
_____	_____
_____	_____
_____	_____

4 Look at activity 3. Write things that Jane *has to / doesn't have to* do.

1 Jane has to be hardworking.

2 _____

3 _____

4 _____

5 (My World) Answer the questions about you.

1 Where did you go on holiday last year?

   We went to _____

2 What did you see and do?

   _____

3 Did you visit a museum?

   _____

4 What do you have to do on holiday?

   _____

5 What don't you have to do on holiday?

   _____

7 Feelings

1 **Read and complete the sentences. Use the words in the box.**

> roedb   yrang   rsspedriu   derasc   rrdieow   sythtri
>
> diter   ctixeetd   ~~ngruhy~~   detresetni

1 I didn't eat breakfast this morning. I'm _____ *hungry* _____ .

2 He didn't drink any juice after the football match. He's _____ .

3 I watched this film last year. I'm _____ .

4 She ran in the sports race. Now she's _____ .

5 I like my Maths lesson. I'm _____ in Maths.

6 My brother ate my ice cream! I'm _____ .

7 He didn't know about his birthday party. He was _____ .

8 She saw a snake in the cave. She was _____ .

9 Ben didn't study for the test. Now he's _____ .

10 We go on holiday tomorrow! I'm _____ .

2 **Look at activity 1. Complete the table about you.**

What feelings do you have when you ... ?

1 cry: *worried,* _____

2 laugh: _____

3 skip: _____

4 shout: _____

5 do homework: _____

My picture dictionary Go to page 91: Write the new words.

3 Write sentences with *because*.

1 She's tired. She's cleaning the house.

She's tired because she's cleaning the house.

2 They're laughing. The book is funny.

_____

3 Ben's scared. He saw a shark.

_____

4 Liam's is shouting. He's angry.

_____

5 We're interested. The story is clever.

_____

6 We're excited. We're going on holiday.

_____

4 Look and write sentences with *because*.

1 (child / crying / dropped his ice cream)
The girl's crying because she dropped her ice cream.

2 (dog / happy / it's eating the ice cream)

_____

_____

3 (Peter / hungry / breakfast time)

_____

4 (Tom / not hungry / tired)

_____

5 (Karen / surprised / kayaking is easy)

_____

6 (Jane / worried / kayaking is difficult)

_____

_____

5 Read and circle the correct words.

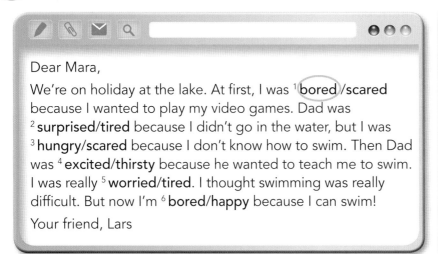

Dear Mara,

We're on holiday at the lake. At first, I was ¹ bored/scared because I wanted to play my video games. Dad was ² surprised/tired because I didn't go in the water, but I was ³ hungry/scared because I don't know how to swim. Then Dad was ⁴ excited/thirsty because he wanted to teach me to swim. I was really ⁵ worried/tired. I thought swimming was really difficult. But now I'm ⁶ bored/happy because I can swim!

Your friend, Lars

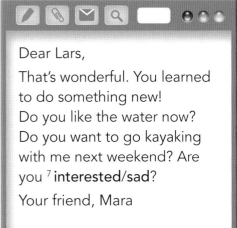

Dear Lars,

That's wonderful. You learned to do something new!
Do you like the water now?
Do you want to go kayaking with me next weekend? Are you ⁷ interested/sad?

Your friend, Mara

6 Put the words in order. Then complete the questions.

1   ___Why___ is Alex laughing? is / he's / Alex / because / watching / laughing / film. / funny / a

Alex is laughing because he's watching a funny film.

2 _____ is Katy hungry? she / hungry / lunch. / eat / She's / because / didn't

_____

3 _____ is Helen _____? because / she / tired / She's / played / volleyball.

_____

4 _____ is he _____? the / he's / excited / to / He's / cinema. / because / going

_____

5 _____ she _____? can / ride / because / a / She's / bike. / happy / she

_____

6 _____ he _____? doesn't / He's / scared / he / because / like / bats.

_____

7 Ask and answer with a friend. Use the words in the box and your own ideas.

happy   ~~tired~~   excited   interested   scared

Why are you tired?   I'm tired because I played football.

8 **Read the story again and complete the sentences with the words in the box. Then number.**

a   Jack needs help because of the _____ .

b   Capu wants to _____ Jack and finds the Annatto plant.

1 c   Capu's excited because he's in ___South America___ .

d   The children say _____ to Capu.

e   The woman and girl use the plant to make a _____ .

> goodbye
> medicine
> snake
> ~~South America~~
> help

9 **Read and circle the correct words.**

1   Capuchin monkeys live in the ... .
a   rainforest   b   home   c   medicine

2   The children are worried and scared because of the ... .
a   rainforest   b   snake   c   Annatto plant

3   What does Capu find on the tablet?
a   his family   b   the Annatto plant   c   snakes

4   The rainforest people make medicine with ... .
a   hospitals   b   snakes   c   plants

5   Why is Capu happy at the end?
a   because he likes medicine   b   because he's hungry   c   because he's home

10 **Read and circle the words that show the value: respect nature.**

1   **Don't throw**/**Throw** bottles in the sea.

2   **Don't take/Take** birds' nests.

3   **Don't put/Put** food in bins at the beach.

4   **Don't make/Make** fires in the forest.

5   **Don't drop/Drop** litter in the forest.

Skills: *Reading*

11 **Read Milt's diary. Then use the underlined words to write sentences with *because*.**

JUNE 6TH	JUNE 7TH
Today was a long day. We flew to Africa. <u>I was bored. The plane ride was ten hours!</u> <u>I'm excited now. We're staying near a national park!</u>	Today we went to the national park. Lions climbed on our car, but we were safe in the car. We also saw hippos in the river. They are so big! <u>I'm surprised. Hippos are the most dangerous. animal.</u> It's not the lion! <u>I'm hungry now. I didn't eat dinner.</u> I was too excited. <u>I want to be a park guide. I am very interested in animals now.</u>

1 I was bored because the plane ride was ten hours. _____

2 _____

3 _____

4 _____

5 _____

12 **Look at activity 11. Answer the questions.**

1 What did Milt do on June 6th? He flew to Africa. _____

2 Did Milt see lions on June 7th? _____

3 Why do you think Milt was safe on June 7th?

_____

4 Are hippos safe animals? _____

5 Why was Milt too excited to eat dinner?

_____

13 **(TIP)** **How to talk about yesterday.**

When we write about yesterday, last week and last year, we sometimes use *was* and *were*: *I was excited.   We were hungry.*

When we write about today, we sometimes use *am*, *is* and *are* with the word *now*: *I'm excited now.   We're hungry now.*

Read Milt's diary again and:

1 circle the sentences with the word *now*.

2 draw boxes around the sentences with *was* and *were*.

Skills: *Writing*

14   Think about your weekend or a holiday. Make notes about two things you did and your feelings.

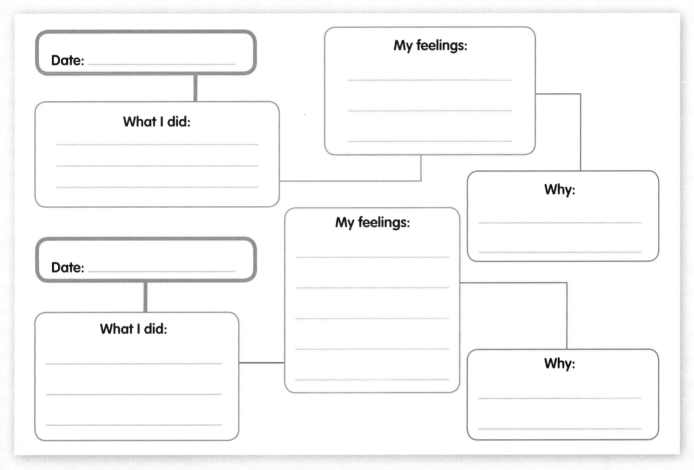

Date: _____

What I did:
_____
_____

My feelings:
_____
_____

Why:
_____
_____

Date: _____

What I did:
_____
_____
_____

My feelings:
_____
_____
_____
_____

Why:
_____
_____

15   Write two diary pages about your weekend or holiday.

Date: _____

Date: _____

How do animals communicate?

1 Match the animals with how they communicate and their feelings.

1	bears	**a**	hiss		excited
2	wild cats	**b**	growl		happy
3	elephants	**c**	flap ears		angry
4	snakes	**d**	move heads		angry
5	polar bears	**e**	purr		happy

2 Look at activity 1. Write sentences about how animals communicate their feelings.

1 _Bears growl because they're angry._

2 _____

3 _____

4 _____

5 _____

3 Complete the table with the words in the box.

See	Hear
change colour	_growl_

~~change colour~~   flap ears ~~growl~~   hiss   purr move fast   move head touch hands

Evaluation

1 Complete the questions and put the words in order. Then match.

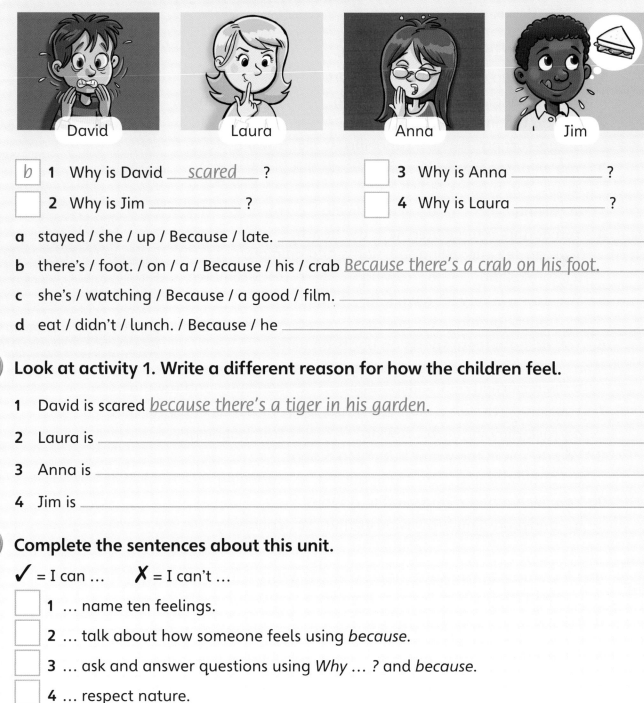

David   Laura   Anna   Jim

b | **1** Why is David ___scared___ ? | **3** Why is Anna _____ ?
  | **2** Why is Jim _____ ? | **4** Why is Laura _____ ?

a stayed / she / up / Because / late. _____

b there's / foot. / on / a / Because / his / crab _Because there's a crab on his foot._

c she's / watching / Because / a good / film. _____

d eat / didn't / lunch. / Because / he _____

2 Look at activity 1. Write a different reason for how the children feel.

1 David is scared _because there's a tiger in his garden._

2 Laura is _____

3 Anna is _____

4 Jim is _____

3 Complete the sentences about this unit.

✓ = I can …   ✗ = I can't …

1 … name ten feelings.

2 … talk about how someone feels using *because*.

3 … ask and answer questions using *Why … ?* and *because*.

4 … respect nature.

5 … talk about my favourite author.

6 The part of this unit I found the most interesting is _____ .

8 Outdoor sports

1 **Read and circle the correct words.**

1 You jump up and down in this sport.
   a canoeing   **b** snorkelling   **c** (trampolining)

2 You do this in a very small car.
   a go-karting   **b** canoeing   **c** rowing

3 You wear special clothes and you do this under the water. You see lots of fish.
   a hiking   **b** scuba diving   **c** rowing

4 You do this in the water, near the beach. You can see interesting sea plants and animals.
   a snorkelling   **b** rowing   **c** rock-climbing

5 You go for a very long walk for this activity.
   a bodyboarding   **b** hiking   **c** windsurfing

6 You do both these sports on boats on water.
   a rock-climbing and go-karting
   b windsurfing and bodyboarding   **c** canoeing and rowing

7 You can do this on a mountain. You use your hands and your feet.
   a rock-climbing   **b** rowing   **c** trampolining

8 You do this in the water but not in a boat.
   a bodyboarding   **b** trampolining   **c** canoeing

9 You need a board and wind to do this.
   a bodyboarding   **b** windsurfing   **c** canoeing

2 **Complete the sentences. Use the words from activity 1 and your own ideas.**

1 I'd like to ____go canoeing____ because _____ .

2 I'd like to _____ because _____ .

3 I'd like to _____ because _____ .

4 I'd like to _____ because _____ .

5 I'd like to _____ because _____ .

My picture dictionary ➔ Go to page 92: Write the new words.

3 Look and write the sentences.

1 (Haley / rowing)   _Haley went rowing on Saturday._
2 (she/ windsurfing)   _____
3 (she / bodyboarding)   _____
4 (Fred / trampolining)   _____
5 (he / go-karting)   _____
6 (they / hiking)   _____

4 Look at activity 3. Complete the questions and write the answers.

1 ___Did___ Haley ___go___ scuba diving?   _No, she didn't._
2 _____ Fred _____ rock-climbing?   _____
3 _____ they _____ bodyboarding?   _____
4 _____ Fred _____ windsurfing?   _____
5 _____ Haley _____ canoeing?   _____

5 (My World) Answer the questions about you.

1 What did you do last Saturday?
   Last Saturday, I _____
2 What did your friend do last weekend?
   _____
3 Did you go hiking last month?
   _____
4 Did you go to school last week?
   _____

6 Read and write the questions and answers.

	January	February	March	April	May
Jen	snowboarding	trampolining	windsurfing	rowing	go-karting

1 Paul: <u>When did you go windsurfing</u> ?

Jen: <u>I went windsurfing in</u> March.

2 Paul: _____ ?

Jen: _____ May.

3 Paul: _____ snowboarding?

Jen: _____ .

4 Paul: _____ rowing?

Jen: _____ .

5 Paul: _____ ?

Jen: _____ February.

	January	February	March	April	May
Eddie	hiking	rock-climbing	windsurfing	canoeing	trampolining

	January	February	March	April	May
Kate	ice-skating	trampolining	rock-climbing	windsurfing	canoeing

7 Read and complete the questions and answers.

Kate: <u>Did</u> you go windsurfing last year?

Eddie: Yes, <u>I did</u> .

Kate: So <u>did I</u> . _____ you _____ windsurfing?

Eddie: In _____ .

Kate: Oh, I _____ windsurfing in _____ .

Eddie: _____ you go canoeing?

Kate: Yes, _____ .

Eddie: So _____ . _____ you go _____ ?

Kate: I _____ in May.

Eddie: I see. I _____ canoeing in _____ .

8 (Think) **Read the story again. Match and then number.**

1	The children are looking for ___e___		a	to be safe.
	It is time for ___		b	go rock-climbing.
	They fly back ___		c	Sofia to go home.
	To get to the helicopter, they must ___		d	to the library.
	They put on helmets ___		e	something to fly.

9 **Use the words in the box to write answers.**

~~helicopter~~   goodbye   rock-climbing   Colombia   the quiz

1 You can fly in this.   _helicopter_

2 You must use ropes and helmets to do this.   _____

3 Sofia comes from this place.   _____

4 The children got all the answers to win this.   _____

5 Sofia, Ruby and Jack say this to each other.   _____

10 (My World) **Find and write sentences that show the value: be safe.**

1 stop / Always / red / the / at / light.
   Always stop at the red light.

2 to / Learn / swim.

   _____

3 bike / Ride / your / slowly.

   _____

4 Don't / your / very / quickly. / food / eat

   _____

11 **Look, read and complete Tony's story. Use the words in the box.**

> bodyboarding   book   ~~swimming~~
> whale watching   swimming   windsurfing

My favourite day,
by Tony

My favourite day happened last July. My family and I went to the beach. My family are all

sportier than me. My dad likes ¹ _swimming_ . My sister likes ² _____ .

My mum always goes ³ _____ . So they did sport and I just read my

⁴ _____ . I was so bored! The beach is not my favourite place.

Then I saw a man. He was really excited and he pointed at the sea. I looked at the sea and

I saw a tail! Then two tails! Then I used the man's special glasses called binoculars.

I saw whales ⁵ _____ in the ocean! I was really excited too. Whales are very

big and very beautiful. They are so cool! Now I'm not bored at the beach because I love

⁶ _____ !

12 **Look at activity 11. Answer the questions.**

1 When did Tony's favourite day happen?
   His favourite day happened last July.

2 What are Tony's family like?
   _____

3 Why was Tony bored?
   _____

4 Why was Tony excited?
   _____

5 Why do you think this was Tony's favourite day?
   _____

13 **(TIP)** **How to use *so*, *very* and *really*.**

Use *so*, *very* and *really* before words to make things bigger and stronger.
Add exclamation marks if you want to:
This cake is really good!   *Tony is so nice!*   *That whale is really big!*

Read Tony's story again and circle the words that make things stronger.

Skills: *Writing*

14   **Think of a time you were *excited* or *interested*. Make notes about it.**

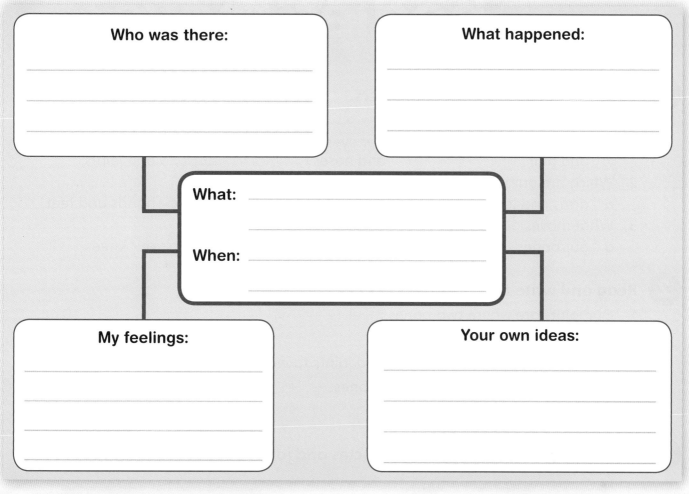

Who was there:

What happened:

What:

When:

My feelings:

Your own ideas:

15 **Write a story about the time you were *excited* or *interested*.**

Title: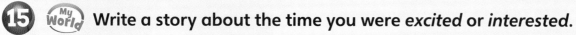

What makes our bodies move?

1 **Read and circle the correct answers.**

1   What makes our bodies move?
   a   our heads, faces and hair
   b   our eyes, ears and noses
   c   (our bones, muscles and joints)

2   Which are our joints?
   a   arms and legs
   b   knees and elbows
   c   hands and feet

3   What moves our joints?
   a   our bones
   b   our muscles
   c   our knees

2 **Read and write *true* or *false*.**

1   Our joints are where two bones meet.   *true*
2   There are no muscles in our legs.   _____
3   We need strong bones, muscles and joints to watch TV.   _____
4   Our knees are between two arm bones.   _____
5   There are muscles in our faces.   _____

3 **Look and think. Which bones, muscles and joints must be strong?**

Arm bones, muscles and elbow joints.

Evaluation

1 **Read and complete. Use the words in the box.**

> didn't   February   hiking
> ~~went~~   windsurfing   When

Tina: Hi, Mike. Guess what! I ¹____went____ to Hawaii.

Mike: So did I. ²_____ did you go to Hawaii?

Tina: I went in ³_____ . It was hot.

Mike: I went in March. It was hotter. Did you
go scuba diving?

Tina: No, I ⁴_____ . I went ⁵_____ .

Mike: Oh, I didn't go windsurfing.
Did you go ⁶_____ ?

Tina: Yes, I did. I went hiking on a volcano!

2 **Look at activity 1. Put the words in order. Then match to the answers.**

1 Tina / When / go / Hawaii? / did / to
When did Tina go to Hawaii?   b

2 Mike / to / in / Did / go / March? / Hawaii
_____

3 the sea? / What / Tina / did / do / in
_____

4 go / Tina / Hawaii? / scuba diving / Did / in
_____

5 do / What / volcano? / Tina / on / did / the
_____

a Yes, he did.

b She went in February.

c She went hiking.

d No, she didn't.

e She went windsurfing.

3 **Complete the sentences about this unit.**

✓ = I can …   ✗ = I can't …

☐ **1** … name ten outdoor sports.

☐ **2** … talk about activities people did last year or last month using *did* and *went*.

☐ **3** … ask and answer questions using *Did … ?* and *When did … ?*

☐ **4** … be safe.

☐ **5** … think and write about an unusual sport and how to play it.

6 My favourite part of this unit was _____ .

Review Units 7 and 8

1 Find and circle the words in the box. Then complete the sentences.

~~rowing~~   go-karting   interested   happy   ~~surprised~~
tired   hiking   sad   snorkelling   windsurfing

1 I'm _surprised_ that I liked ___rowing___ .
Usually I don't like boats. And I didn't like
canoeing.

2 Iris was _____ last Friday because
she didn't go _____ . She likes
driving the little cars.

3 Mark wants to go _____ . He is
_____ because he likes fish. He liked
scuba diving, but he wants to try a
new sport.

4 I'm _____ because I went
_____ . I think it's more difficult
than surfing or body-boarding! I was
excited because of the wind.

5 Jill is _____ because she went
_____ on a mountain. She
wants to go to bed.

S	N	O	R	K	E	L	L	I	N	G
G	O	K	A	R	T	I	N	G	F	X
B	H	A	P	P	Y	A	S	A	D	T
W	I	Z	R	H	I	K	I	N	G	Y
N	A	N	J	G	R	O	W	I	N	G
Z	S	U	R	P	R	I	S	E	D	D
T	I	N	T	E	R	E	S	T	E	D
X	T	I	R	E	D	Y	F	G	E	V
W	I	N	D	S	U	R	F	I	N	G

2 Read and match.

1 They're laughing … | g |
2 Nina is surprised … | |
3 Why is Leon worried? | |
4 Why is Mary excited? | |
5 We didn't go … | |
6 What did Kyla do last Friday? | |
7 When did they go swimming? | |

a Because he didn't study.
b She went trampolining.
c They went last spring.
d because there's a rabbit in the hat.
e Because it's her birthday.
f go-karting last Sunday.
g because the story is funny.

Read and answer the questions.

Four friends did four different activities last July:
Henry didn't go hiking, rock-climbing or bodyboarding.
Nancy didn't go rock-climbing, canoeing or hiking.
Mick didn't go canoeing, rock-climbing or bodyboarding.
Ellen didn't go bodyboarding, canoeing or hiking.
The person who went canoeing was scared.
The person who went bodyboarding was excited.
The person who went rock-climbing was interested.
The person who went hiking was happy.

1 Did Henry go rock-climbing last July?

No, he didn't. He went canoeing.

2 Did Nancy go bodyboarding last July?

3 What did Mick do last July?

4 What did Ellen do last July?

5 Who was scared last July? Why?

6 Who was excited last July? Why?

 Answer the questions about you.

1 What are you feeling now and why?
I'm feeling

2 Is your friend happy? Why or why not?

3 What did you do last December?

4 Do you like swimming in the sea?

5 What activities would you like to do?

83

Around the world

Brazil

artistic

cry

crab

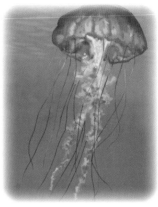

4 Gadgets

digital camera

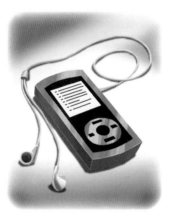

5 The natural world

cave

clean the bathroom

7 Feelings

angry

bodyboarding

_____

_____

_____

_____

_____

_____

_____

_____

_____

Story fun

1 Who said it? Read and write the names.

Jack   Ruby   Sofia

1   _Sofia_   Oh, no! I don't like bats.

2   _____   It's 1950. Look at this diary.

3   _____   And look at this! It's a message.

4   _____   It was the key.

5   _____   OK, but we must be safe. Put on your helmets and follow me.

6   _____   And look! It's the monkey!

7   _____   Quick! Help me find some shells.

8   _____   Yes! They made a medicine with the plant.

9   _____   My penpal, Sofia, is from Colombia! We can email her.

2 Look at the pictures and write the values.

> Encourage your friends.   Use technology wisely.   Learn about other cultures.
> Be kind to animals.   Help other people.   ~~Be safe~~

1

Be safe.

2

3

4

5

6

Look and complete the word puzzle.

Across

1 Do trees grow in Antarctica?

2 Which city in Colombia has a flower festival?

3 Where does the Annatto plant grow?

Down

4 Where are capuchin monkeys from?

5 Which country is Hollywood in?

6 Which river flows through Egypt?

7 What is a dolphin family called?

Thanks and Acknowledgements

The authors and publishers would like to thank the following contributors:
Blooberry Design: concept design, book design, page make-up
Bridget Kelly: editing

The authors and publishers acknowledge the following sources of copyright material and are grateful for the permissions granted. While every effort has been made, it has not always been possible to identify the sources of all the material used, or to trace all copyright holders. If any omissions are brought to our notice, we will be happy to include the appropriate acknowledgements on reprinting.

The authors and publishers would like to thank the following illustrators:

Pablo Gallego (Beehive Illustration): pp. 3, 7, 15, 23, 33, 41, 51, 59, 69, 77, 93, 94, 95; Mark Duffin: pp. 4, 55, 75; Paul Williams (Syvie Poggio): pp. 19, 33; Timo Grubbing (Beehive): pp. 26, 67; Dusan Pavlic (Beehive): pp. 27, 31, 56, 73; Simon Walmesley: pp. 29, 63; Ilias Arahovitis (Beehive): pp. 30, 60; Humberto Blanco (Sylvie Poggio): pp. 64, 78; Brian Lee: pp. 36, 62, 70; Richard Jones (Beehive): p. 37; Niall Harding (Beehive): p. 54; Gustavo Berardo (Beehive): p. 58; Hardinge (Monkey Feet): pp. 84, 85, 86, 87, 88, 89, 90, 91, 92.

The authors and publishers would like to thank the following for permission to reproduce photographs:

p. 4 (opener): Tim Gainey/Alamy; p. 5 (1): Digital Media Pro/Shutterstock; p. 5 (2): Blend Images/Shutterstock; p. 5 (3): JGI/Tom Grill/Corbis; p. 5 (4): Kamira/Shutterstock; p. 6: Tony Garcia/Corbis; p. 7: imageBROKER/Alamy; p. 8 (T): Basque Country - Mark Baynes/Alamy; p. 8 (B): Geoffrey Robinson/Alamy; p. 10 (opener): John Dunne/Getty; p. 10 (a): BRUCE COLEMAN INC./Alamy; p. 10 (b): Sue Martin/Alamy; p. 10 (c): Dario Sabljak/Shutterstock; p. 11: Jaren Jai Wicklund/Shutterstock; p. 12 (opener): Wilfried Martin/Getty; p. 12 (TR): VP Photo Studio/Shutterstock; p. 12 (1): H. Mark Weidman Photography/Alamy; p. 12 (2): PathDoc/Shutterstock; p. 12 (3): oliveromg/Shutterstock; p. 12 (4): Wavebreak Media LTD/Corbis; p. 13 (TL): Donna Ellen Coleman/Shutterstock; p. 13 (TR): Brocreative/Shutterstock; p. 14: Muellek Josef/Shutterstock; p. 15: John Warburton-Lee Photography/Alamy; p. 16 (T): Volodymyr Burdiak/Shutterstock; p. 16 (B): Dorothy Alexander/Alamy; p. 18 (opener): TeguhSantosa/Getty; p. 18 (a): Nature Picture Library/Alamy; p. 18 (b): david tipling/Alamy; p. 18 (c): Christina Krutz/Corbis; p. 20 (opener): J. McPhail/Shutterstock; p. 20 (a): Grady Reese/Corbis; p. 20 (b): Alex Segre/Alamy; p. 20 (c): Paul Springett 02/Alamy; p. 20 (d): Bokhach/Shutterstock; p. 20 (e): Giulio_Fornasar/Shutterstock; p. 20 (f): SergiyN/Shutterstock; p. 21: Agencja Fotograficzna Caro/Alamy; p. 22 (T): Ronnie Kaufman/Larry Hirshowitz/Corbis; p. 22 (B): Hero Images Inc./Alamy; p. 23: Markus Mainka/Shutterstock; p. 24: luminaimages/Shutterstock; p. 28 (a): takayuki/Shutterstock; p. 28 (b): Susan Schmitz/Shutterstock; p. 28 (c): Cristian Zamfir/Shutterstock; p. 28 (d): S Curtis/Shutterstock; p. 30 (opener): Michael Moxter/Getty; p. 30 (1): Jason Edwards/Getty; p. 30 (2): David Osborn/Alamy; p. 30 (3): Bryce R. Bradford/Getty; p. 30 (4): Steve Hamblin/Alamy; p. 30 (5): James Azzurro/Alamy; p. 32 (a): Johan Swanepoel/Shutterstock; p. 32 (b): davemhuntphotography/Shutterstock; p. 32 (c): imageBROKER/Alamy; p. 32 (d): Maros Bauer/Shutterstock; p. 34: Egill Bjarnason/Alamy; p. 36 (opener): Zac Macaulay/Corbis; p. 38 (opener): Scott Stulberg/Corbis; p. 38 (T): Ralko/Shutterstock; p. 38 (B): Andersen Ross/Getty; p. 39 (1): wavebreakmedia/Shutterstock; p. 39 (2): Fotokostic/Shutterstock; p. 39 (3): Happy person/Shutterstock; p. 39 (4): Pauline St. Denis/Corbis; p. 39 (5): gorillaimages/Shutterstock; p. 39 (6): holbox/Shutterstock; p. 40 (T): Sergey Novikov/Shutterstock; p. 40 (B): www.saint-tropez-photo.com/Getty; p. 41: Andresr/Shutterstock; p. 42 (1): Science Museum/Science and Society Picture Library; p. 42 (2): Science & Society Picture Library/Getty; p. 44: All Canada Photos/Alamy; p. 45: Ruslan Guzov/Shutterstock; p. 46 (1): Isabelle Kuehn/Shutterstock; p. 46 (2): Steve Noakes/Shutterstock; p. 46 (3): igor.stevanovic/Shutterstock; p. 46 (4): Andaman/Shutterstock; p. 46 (4): Stefan Pircher/Shutterstock; p. 46 (5): Photoshot Holdings Ltd/Alamy; p. 46 (6): imageBROKER/Alamy; p. 48 (opener): George Steinmetz/Corbis; p. 48 (T): Calin Tatu/Shutterstock; p. 48 (B): VVO/Shutterstock; p. 49 (TL): bikeriderlondon/Shutterstock; p. 49 (TR): gorillaimages/Shutterstock; p. 50: KayaMe/Shutterstock; p. 51: MANDY GODBEHEAR/Shutterstock; p. 52 (T): Whit Richardson/Alamy; p. 52 (B): Holger Leue/Getty; p. 54: Corey Ford/Stocktrek Images/Getty; p. 56: Jupiterimages/Getty; p. 57 (T): Yarinca/Getty; p. 57 (B): Blend Images - KidStock/Getty; p. 59: Blend Images/Alamy; p. 62: Weyers, L./Corbis; p. 64 (1): VVO/Shutterstock; p. 64 (2): Janne Hamalainen/Shutterstock; p. 64 (3): Galyna Andrushko/Shutterstock; p. 64 (4): Marques/Shutterstock; p. 64 (5): Petr Kopka/Shutterstock; p. 64 (6): Catmando/Shutterstock; p. 64 (7): haraldmuc/Shutterstock; p. 64 (8): Kevin Eaves/Shutterstock; p. 64 (9): Jason Patrick Ross/Shutterstock; p. 66 (opener): Chad Slattery/Getty; p. 66 (B): Brand New Images/Getty; p. 67 (TR) Pete Pahham/Shutterstock; p. 69: Blend Images/Alamy; p. 72 (opener): Randy Wells/Corbis; p. 72 (BR): Roblan/Shutterstock; p. 74 (opener): mountainberryphoto/Getty; p. 74 (BR): Jeremy Pembrey/Alamy; p. 77: Beth Swanson/Shutterstock; p. 80 (opener): John P Kelly/Getty; p. 80 (1): BSIP SA/Alamy; p. 80 (2): CroMary/Shutterstock; p. 80 (3): Aurora Photos/Alamy; p. 80 (4): Arthur Tilley/Getty; p. 81: tomas del amo/Shutterstock; p. 82: Hero Images/Corbis; p. 83: Philip Quirk/Alamy.

Front Cover photo by aghezzi/Getty Images